yachtmaster

Written by Penny Haire
Illustrations by Sarah Selman

www.rya.org.uk

Royal Yachting Association
RYA House, Ensign Way, Hamble, Southampton SO31 4YA
Tel: 0845 345 0400 Fax: 0845 345 0329
email: training@rya.org.uk website: www.rya.org.uk

Produced by: AVALON DESIGN+PRINT • Christchurch • Dorset

CONTENTS

Charts reproduced throughout this book are for training purposes only. On no account should they be used for navigation.

Navigational Charts

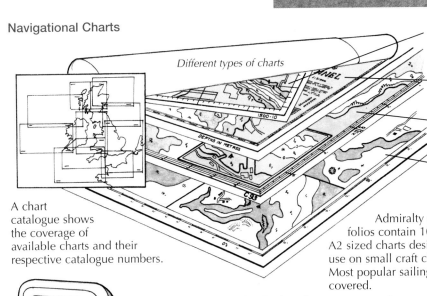

Different types of charts

Admiralty Small Craft Edition

Admiralty Standard Edition

Imray

Stanford

A chart catalogue shows the coverage of available charts and their respective catalogue numbers.

Electronic charts can be displayed on a dedicated plotter or a PC.

Updates for some types are available on disk or CD ROM making them easy to correct. Be aware that the quality, detail and coverage of electronic charts varies widely.

Admiralty small craft folios contain 10 or more A2 sized charts designed for use on small craft chart tables. Most popular sailing areas are covered.

Keep your charts up to date by making minor corrections. Details of these are found in Admiralty 'Notices to Mariners'.

You may have to replace a chart if major corrections are needed - usually a new edition of a chart is produced instead.

Nautical Almanacs and Pilot books

Publications giving notes on pilotage can greatly enhance the information gleaned from a chart. They can give:
Aerial photos, detailed pilotage notes and sketches, local information/town plans etc.

Be aware that information from pilotage publications can be out of date and is not a substitute for a fully corrected chart.

Small craft almanacs give a large amount of extremely useful infomation such as:

Tidal heights and streams.

Pilotage and passage planning information.

Weather information.

3

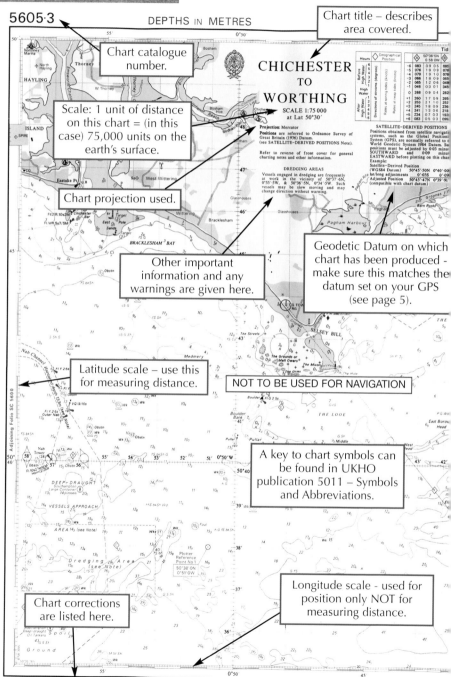

5605·3 — DEPTHS IN METRES

Chart title – describes area covered.

Chart catalogue number.

CHICHESTER TO WORTHING
SCALE 1:75 000
at Lat 50°30'

Scale: 1 unit of distance on this chart = (in this case) 75,000 units on the earth's surface.

Chart projection used.

Other important information and any warnings are given here.

Geodetic Datum on which chart has been produced - make sure this matches the datum set on your GPS (see page 5).

Latitude scale – use this for measuring distance.

NOT TO BE USED FOR NAVIGATION

A key to chart symbols can be found in UKHO publication 5011 – Symbols and Abbreviations.

Longitude scale - used for position only NOT for measuring distance.

Chart corrections are listed here.

5605·3

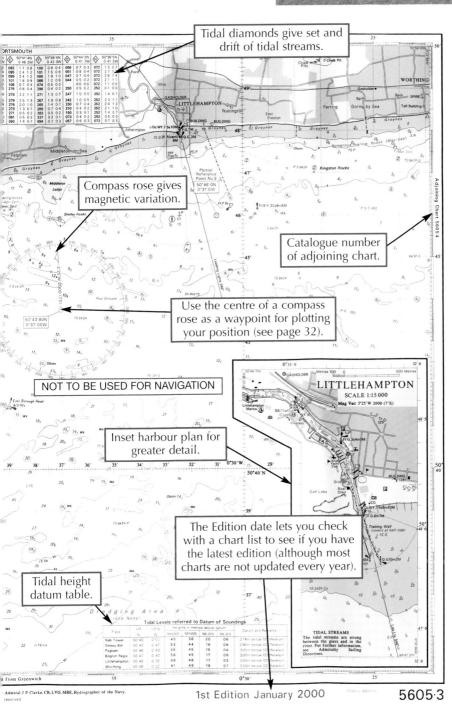

Tidal diamonds give set and drift of tidal streams.

Compass rose gives magnetic variation.

Catalogue number of adjoining chart.

Use the centre of a compass rose as a waypoint for plotting your position (see page 32).

NOT TO BE USED FOR NAVIGATION

Inset harbour plan for greater detail.

The Edition date lets you check with a chart list to see if you have the latest edition (although most charts are not updated every year).

Tidal height datum table.

1st Edition January 2000

5605·3

5

Latitude and Longitude

Lines of Longitude, called Meridians, run from pole to pole dividing the earth into segments rather like an orange.

Lines of Latitude, called Parallels, are obtained by projecting angles made from the centre of the earth to points on its surface.

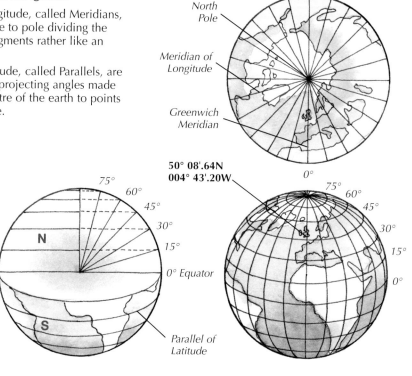

Parallel of Latitude

Plotting your position

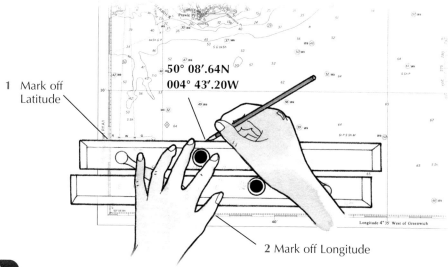

1 Mark off Latitude

50° 08'.64N
004° 43'.20W

2 Mark off Longitude

Range and bearing

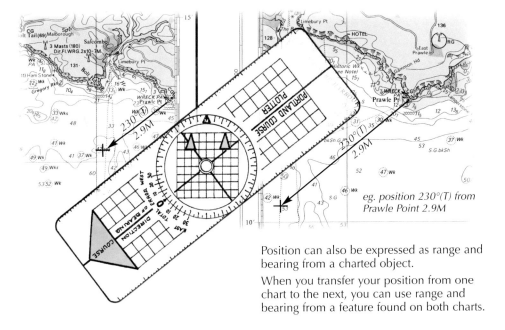

eg. position 230°(T) from Prawle Point 2.9M

Position can also be expressed as range and bearing from a charted object.

When you transfer your position from one chart to the next, you can use range and bearing from a feature found on both charts.

GEODETIC DATUMS

Latitude and Longitude are derived from a reference at the earth's centre, but the earth is not a true sphere so different datums must be used which are appropriate for different parts of the world.

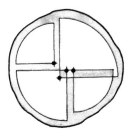

This is a position in the Dover Strait, plotted using different datums.

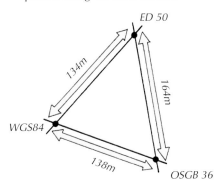

Satellite derived positions are normally referred to WGS 84 datum. It is possible to change this within the setup of a GPS.

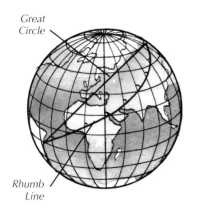

Great Circle

Rhumb Line

Chart projections are an attempt to represent the curved surface ot the earth on a flat piece of paper.

The shortest distance between two points on the earth's surface is on a Great Circle route.

If you sail an unchanging course you will cut the Parallels of Longitude at equal angles, this is known as a Rhumb Line route. You sail a slightly longer distance using a Rhumb Line route but this is only really significant on a long ocean passage.

The most useful chart for practical use is one where a Rhumb Line is shown as a straight line.

Mercator projection

In order to represent a Rhumb Line as a straight line, the meridians have to be made parallel. This stretches land masses at the top of a chart in an east-west direction, so to keep them the correct shape they must also be stretched in a north-south direction.

The scale gradually increases towards the top of the chart,

this is why you must always measure distance on the Latitude scale opposite your position.

Rhumb Line

Most UKHO charts and Ordnance Survey maps are constructed using a Transverse Mercator projection.

Gnomonic projection

This projection is mainly used for planning ocean passages, as a great circle route is shown as a straight line.

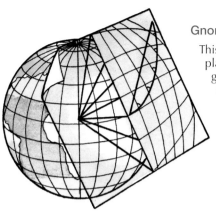

DISTANCE

1° Latitude = 60' (minutes)

1' = 60" (seconds)

1 minute of Latitude = 1 sea mile

We use tenths of a minute, not seconds for chart work e.g. 50°17'.4N

0.1 sea mile = 1 cable = 185m (approx)

The length of a sea mile varies slightly with Latitude so for practical purposes we use the nautical mile which is fixed in length.

A knot is one nautical mile per hour.

NOTATION OF BEARINGS

1 kilometre
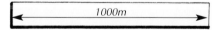
1000m

1 statute (land) mile

1609m

1 nautical mile
1852m

MAGNETIC VARIATION

Charts show North as True (Geographic) North. A compass can only point to magnetic North, the difference between the two is called *variation*.

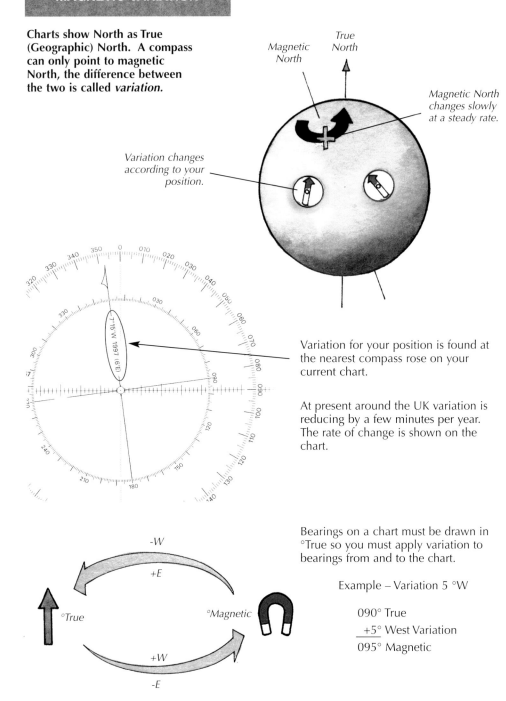

Magnetic North changes slowly at a steady rate.

Variation changes according to your position.

Variation for your position is found at the nearest compass rose on your current chart.

At present around the UK variation is reducing by a few minutes per year. The rate of change is shown on the chart.

Bearings on a chart must be drawn in °True so you must apply variation to bearings from and to the chart.

Example – Variation 5 °W

090° True
+5° West Variation
095° Magnetic

Ferrous metal and magnetic fields will affect the compass, for instance: engine, instruments, cockpit speakers and mobile phones.

When the boat's heading changes – deviation changes.

You can check deviation by lining up on a charted transit and comparing heading with the true bearing of the transit.

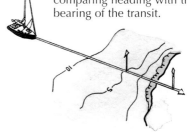

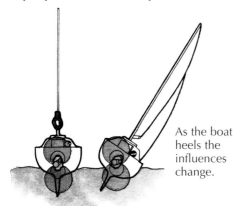

As the boat heels the influences change.

Deviation card

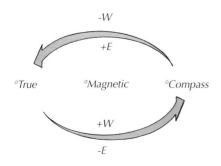

°True   °Magnetic   °Compass

A deviation card can be produced for your steering compass which will show the East or West error on each heading. Use this to convert to °C to °M and vice versa.

SHIPS HEAD°(C)	DEVIATION
000°	4° W
022½	2° W
045	0°
067½	2° E
090	4° E
112½	5° E
135	6° E
157½	5° E
180	4° E
202½	2° E
225	0°
247½	2° W
270	4° W
292½	5° W
315	6° W
337½	5° W
360	4° W

Practical application

It is preferable to have your steering compass corrected to eliminate deviation. However, you may be sailing on an unfamiliar boat such as a charter boat or on a delivery trip. In this situation is always wise to check for deviation and apply it as necessary.

Be aware that even in a moderate sea it is difficult to steer a very precise course.

This means you may decide to ignore small amounts of deviation.

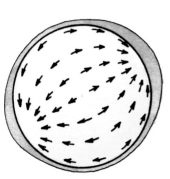

Gravitational pull from the moon and sun is the main cause of tides.

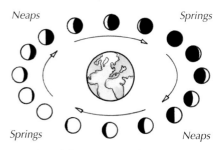

Neaps ... *Springs*

Springs ... *Neaps*

The tidal cycle is 28 days – the period of one full moon to the next.

Spring Tides

When the gravitational pull from the moon and sun are in line, we experience

- high high waters
- low low waters

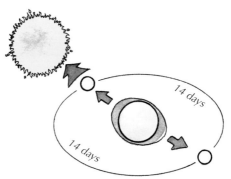

14 days

14 days

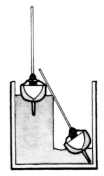

Greater range of tide

Neap Tides

When the gravitational pull from the moon and sun are at right angles to each other, we experience

- low high waters
- high low waters

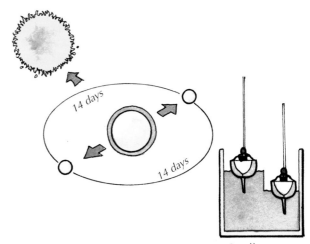

14 days

14 days

Smaller range of tide

Rule of 12ths => 1/12/hr
1/12② 2/12③ 3/12④ 3/12⑤ 2/12⑥ 1/12

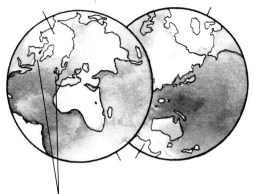

Tidal patterns round the world are quite complex due to the effects of:

- funnelling e.g. into the mouth of the Bristol Channel
- the spin of the earth
- the differing geography of ocean basins
- shallow water.

The Mediterranean and Baltic Seas have negligible tide, mainly because of restrictions at their entrance.

Biggest tidal range in the world is in Canada – the Bay of Fundy (mean range 13m). The second biggest is in the Bristol Channel - 12m.

Effects of the weather

Strong winds for prolonged periods can:

Hold water back making the tidal height greater than predicted.

Push water out making the tidal height less than expected.

Barometric pressure can:

Make the tidal height less than predicted.

Make the tidal height greater than predicted.

Tidal terms

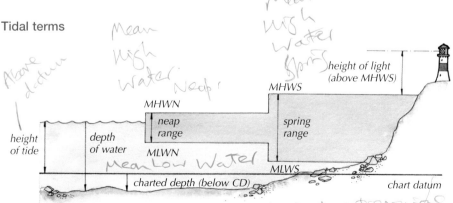

Mean High Water

Mean High Water Neap

Mean High Water Spring

Above datum

height of light (above MHWS)

MHWS

MHWN

neap range

spring range

MLWN

Mean Low Water

MLWS

height of tide

depth of water

charted depth (below CD)

chart datum

true Depth
CD + Height of tide
charted depth .

Lowest astronomical tide LAT

13

Standard ports – tide tables are produced for larger ports and give times and heights of high and low water for every day of the year

HW height

LW height

MARCH			APRIL				
Time	m		Time	m		Time	m
16 0245	(4.8)	**1**	0354	4.9	**16**	0422	(5.3)
0917	(1.4)		1013	1.3		1047	(0.6)
SA 1526	4.8		M 1621	4.9		TU 1651	5.3
2148	1.3		2231	1.3		2309	0.6
17 0350	5.2	**2**	0437	5.1	**17**	0509	5.5
1018	0.9		1054	1.1		1132	0.4
SU 1624	5.1		TU 1703	5.1		W 1735	5.4
2243	0.8		2312	1.0	●	2353	0.4

For summer time add 1 hr in non-shaded area

To find out if a certain day is on springs or neaps subtract LW from HW to give the range:

5.3m - 0.6m = 4.7m

Springs occur 2 to 3 days after a full or new moon

Compare with mean range on curve. Tues 16th April = springs

Tidal curves

Use these for finding out depth of water at any time between high and low water

Rule of Kraths.

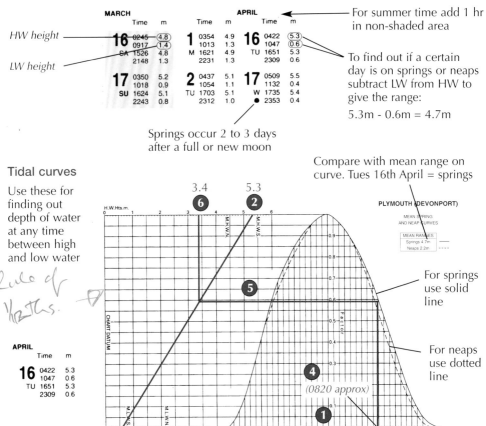

APRIL		
Time	m	
16 0422	5.3	
1047	0.6	
TU 1651	5.3	
2309	0.6	

For springs use solid line

For neaps use dotted line

(0820 approx)

e.g. What will be the height of tide at 0820 on Tues 16th April?

1 enter HW height (local time) and fill in the boxes for each hour after HW

2 + **3** mark in the heights of HW and LW and draw a line between them

4 find 0820 on bottom scale

5 draw line upwards to hit the curve, across to meet the HW/LW line then up to the HW scale

6 there will be **3.4m at 0820**

You can also find out when there will be a specific depth - ie at what time will there be 3.4m height of tide?

Go down to the HW/LW line from the HW scale, across to the curve and down to the time scale = 0820

Example

On the evening of July 21st, at what time will a yacht of 1.8m draft be able to cross the sill at Victoria Marina (St Peter Port Guernsey) with 0.5m clearance? The sill dries 4.4m

HW = 2248 BST 8.1m LW = 1652 2.6m Range = 5.5m (midway between springs and neaps)

Depth of water (above CD) required = 1.8 + 0.5 + 4.4 = <u>6.7m</u>

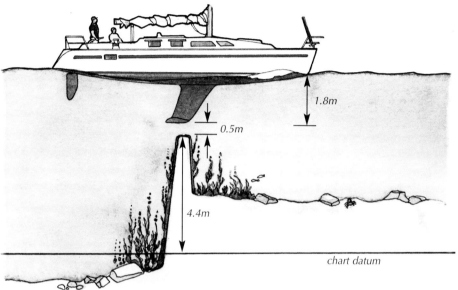

From the curve:
Time at which the depth of water will reach 6.7m = 2058 BST

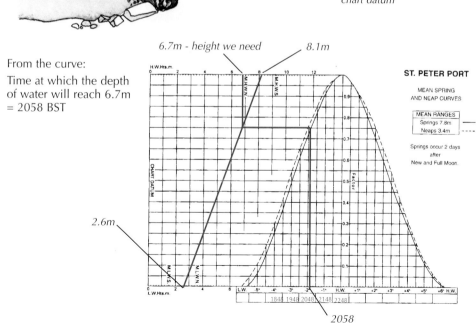

15

SECONDARY PORTS

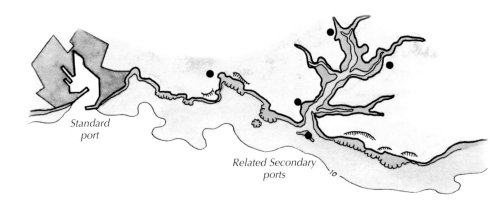

Standard port

Related Secondary ports

Tide tables are normally produced only for standard ports, they tend to be the busier commercial harbours.

A secondary port is a minor port, anchorage, or location such as the entrace to a river. Each is related to a nearby standard port as the tidal heights and times are similar.

We can make corrections to standard port tidal information to give accurate tidal predictions for a secondary port.

Information about secondary port corrections is found in Nautical Almanacs.

Corrections

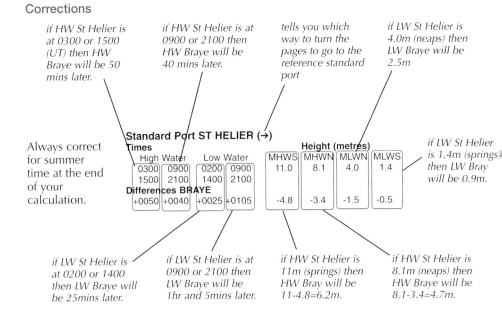

if HW St Helier is at 0300 or 1500 (UT) then HW Braye will be 50 mins later.

if HW St Helier is at 0900 or 2100 then HW Braye will be 40 mins later.

tells you which way to turn the pages to go to the reference standard port

if LW St Helier is 4.0m (neaps) then LW Braye will be 2.5m

Always correct for summer time at the end of your calculation.

Standard Port ST HELIER (→)				Height (metres)			
Times				MHWS	MHWN	MLWN	MLWS
High Water		Low Water					
0300	0900	0200	0900	11.0	8.1	4.0	1.4
1500	2100	1400	2100				
Differences BRAYE							
+0050	+0040	+0025	+0105	-4.8	-3.4	-1.5	-0.5

if LW St Helier is 1.4m (springs) then LW Bray will be 0.9m.

if LW St Helier is at 0200 or 1400 then LW Braye will be 25mins later.

if LW St Helier is at 0900 or 2100 then LW Braye will be 1hr and 5mins later.

if HW St Helier is 11m (springs) then HW Bray will be 11-4.8=6.2m.

if HW St Helier is 8.1m (neaps) then HW Braye will be 8.1-3.4=4.7m.

To make corrections when in between springs and neaps: You must *interpolate* - you can estimate the differences but if you need more accuracy - draw a graph

Example:

St Helier 0445 9.2
       1050 3.2

What are the times and heights for Braye?

HW (0445) falls between
0300 + 0900

LW(1050) falls between
0900 + 1400

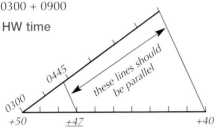

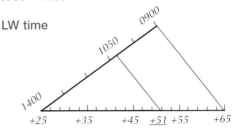

HW Bray = 0445 + 47
        = 0532 UT
        = 0632 BST

To find the height of tide between HW & LW put the secondary port HW height and times on the *standard port curve*.

LW Braye = 1050 + 51
         = 1141 UT
         = 1241 BST

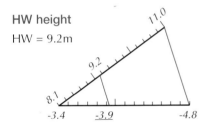

HW height

HW = 9.2m

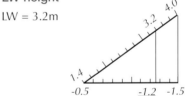

LW height

LW = 3.2m

HW Braye = 9.2 - 3.9
         = 5.3m

LW Braye = 3.2 - 1.2
         = 2.0m

TIDAL ANOMALIES

In some places, for instance in the Solent, the time of HW is not well defined. In these cases if you need to find the time or height of tide between HW & LW use a curve based on LW.

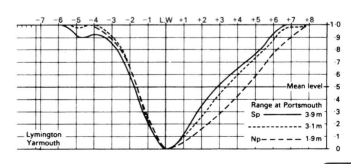

17

Example

Thursday 6th June the weather is fine and calm and you decide to lunch at the small French port of Goury. The boat draws 1.2m, the intended berth dries 4.4m and you want a minimum of 1m under the keel.

Between what times (French Summer Time) can you remain at the berth?

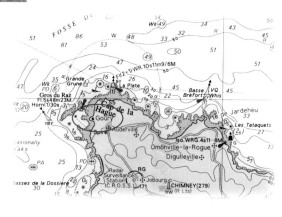

6 0633 1.0 Cherbourg
1211 6.0 Thursday
TH 1856 1.5 6th June

Range = 6.0 - 1.5
= 4.5
25% from springs towards neaps

Standard Port CHERBOURG (←)

Times				Height (metres)			
High Water		Low Water		MHWS	MHWN	MLWN	MLWS
0300	1000	0400	1000	6.4	5.0	2.5	1.1
1500	2200	1600	2200				
Differences OMONVILLE							
-0025	-0030	-0022	-0022	-0.3	-0.2	-0.2	-0.1
GOURY							
-0100	-0040	-0105	-0120	+1.7	+1.6	+1.0	+0.3

Height of tide needed
1.2 + 1.0 + 4.4
= 6.6m

HW time

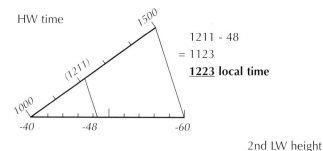

1211 - 48
= 1123
1223 local time

HW height
6.0 + 1.7
= **7.7m**

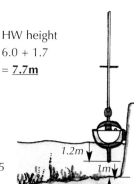

2nd LW height

1.5 + 0.5
= **2.0m**

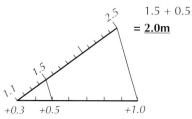

1st LW height
1.0 + 0.3
= **1.3m**

CHERBOURG

MEAN SPRING
AND NEAP CURVES

MEAN RANGES	
Springs 5.3m	———
Neaps 2.5m	- - - -

Springs occur 2 days
after
New and Full Moon.

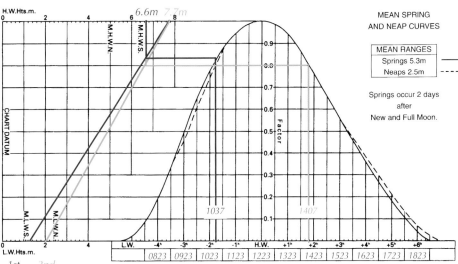

H.W.Hts.m.

6.6m 7.7m

M.H.W.N. M.H.W.S.

CHART DATUM

M.L.W.S. M.L.W.N.

Factor

1037   1407

0 2 4 L.W. -4ʰ -3ʰ -2ʰ -1ʰ H.W. +1ʰ +2ʰ +3ʰ +4ʰ +5ʰ +6ʰ
L.W.Hts.m.

| 0823 | 0923 | 1023 | 1123 | 1223 | 1323 | 1423 | 1523 | 1623 | 1723 | 1823 |

1st   2nd
1.3m   2.0m

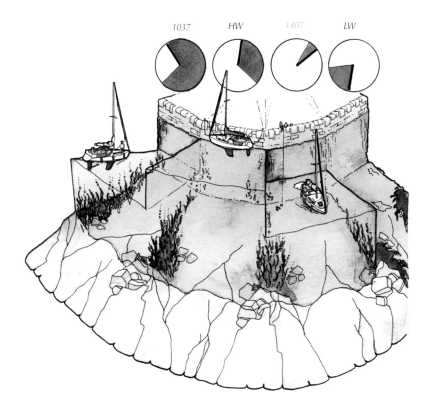

1037   HW   1407   LW

Consider the tidal stream as a travelator

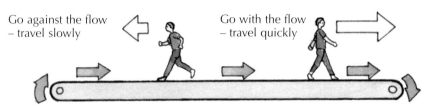

Go against the flow
– travel slowly

Go with the flow
– travel quickly

If you travel across the tidal
stream the boat will be
pushed sideways giving a
different ground track to the
course you are steering

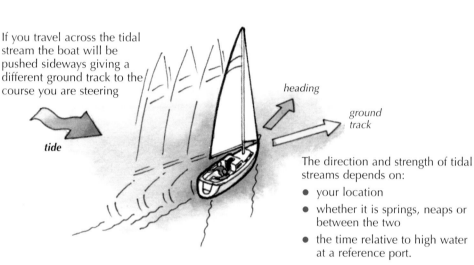

heading

*ground
track*

tide

The direction and strength of tidal
streams depends on:

- your location
- whether it is springs, neaps or
  between the two
- the time relative to high water
  at a reference port.

FINDING THE STRENGTH AND DIRECTION OF THE TIDE

Tidal stream atlas

*direction
(measure with
plotter)*

*spring rate
07 = 0.7kn*

*neap rate
03 = 0.3kn*

time ——— 1 hour before HW Plymouth
(6 hours after HW Dover)

Tidal diamond

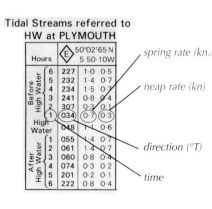

**Tidal Streams referred to
HW at PLYMOUTH**

	Hours	50°02'65 N 5 50·10W	*spring rate (kn)*	*neap rate (kn)*
Before High Water	6	227	1·0	0·5
	5	232	1·4	0·7
	4	234	1·5	0·7
	3	241	0·8	0·4
	2	307	0·3	0·1
	1	034	0·7	0·3
High Water		048	1·1	0·6
After High Water	1	055	1·4	0·7
	2	061	1·4	0·7
	3	060	0·8	0·4
	4	074	0·3	0·2
	5	201	0·2	0·1
	6	222	0·8	0·4

direction (°T)

time

Example

What is the rate and direction of the tidal stream at a position near Plymouth at 0815 BST on Fri 23rd Aug?

1 Find the time of HW and the heights of HW & LW at Plymouth on Fri 23rd Aug

	Time	m
23	0505	1.9
	(1135)	4.5
F	1758	2.0
24	0009	4.4
	0649	2.0
SA	1258	4.5

1135 UT
1235 BST is the nearest HW to 0815

2 Is it springs, neaps or in between?

$$4.5 - 1.9$$
range   2.6m

= neaps (more or less)

3 How many hours before or after HW is 0815?

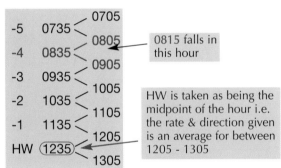

-5   0735 ⟨ 0705 / 0805
-4   0835 ⟨ 0805 / 0905
-3   0935 ⟨ 0905 / 1005
-2   1035 ⟨ 1005 / 1105
-1   1135 ⟨ 1105 / 1205
HW (1235) ⟨ 1205 / 1305

0815 falls in this hour

HW is taken as being the midpoint of the hour i.e. the rate & direction given is an average for between 1205 - 1305

4 Find the nearest ◇ to your position = ⟨C⟩

Spring rate   = 2.3kn
Neap rate   = 1.1kn
Direction of tidal stream = 278°(T)

- 4hrs

HW

◇	50°12′55N 5 05·00W	
277	1·9	1·0
280	2·3	1·1
(278	2·3	1·1)
279	1·7	0·8
296	0·6	0·3
063	0·8	0·4
(081	1·9	0·9)
083	2·2	1·1
077	2·2	1·1
070	1·9	0·9
055	1·0	0·5
310	0·5	0·3
280	1·4	0·7

5 Or using a tidal stream atlas which is the nearest arrow?

4 hours before HW Plymouth
(3 hours after HW Dover)

Spring rate   = 2.3
Neap rate   = 1.1kn
Measure direction of arrow = 278°(T)

Tidal races often form off headlands and the sea can be very rough and disturbed here.

It is often perfectly safe to negotiate a headland in calm conditions and/or at slack water – check your almanac or pilot book for passage information.

Plan your passage to avoid the worst of the rough water.

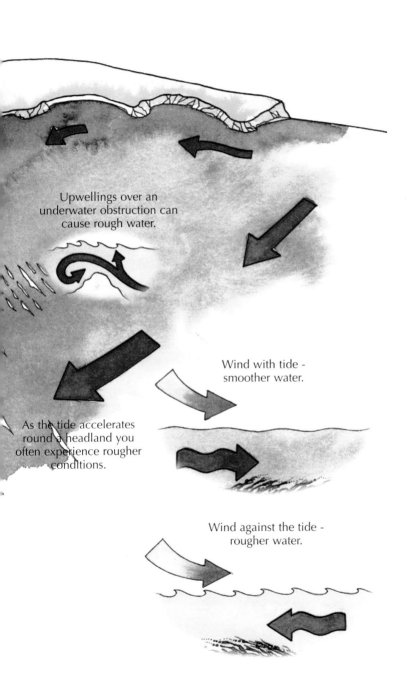

Upwellings over an underwater obstruction can cause rough water.

As the tide accelerates round a headland you often experience rougher conditions.

Wind with tide - smoother water.

Wind against the tide - rougher water.

It is possible to reckon your approx position
if you know:

- the course steered
- distance travelled (measured by log)

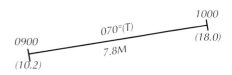

time	log	course
0900	10.2	070°(T)
1000	18.0	070°(T)

(7.8 miles travelled)

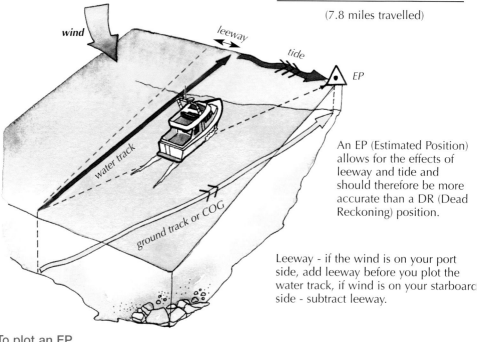

An EP (Estimated Position)
allows for the effects of
leeway and tide and
should therefore be more
accurate than a DR (Dead
Reckoning) position.

Leeway - if the wind is on your port
side, add leeway before you plot the
water track, if wind is on your starboard
side - subtract leeway.

To plot an EP

time	log	course	leeway	wind	tide
0900	10.2	077°(M)	5°	N6	140°(T) 1.4kn
1000	18.0	077°(M)	5°	N6	120°(T) 2.0kn tide for 0900-1000

Water track   = 077°(M)
Variation 7°W   = 070° (T)
Leeway +5°   = 075° (T)

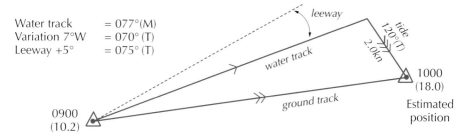

The accuracy of an EP depends on:

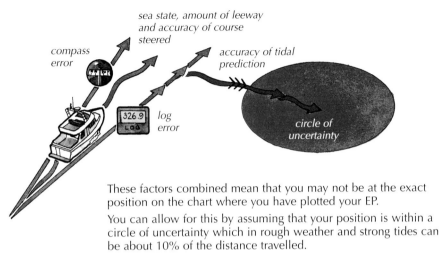

compass error

sea state, amount of leeway and accuracy of course steered

accuracy of tidal prediction

326.9 log error

circle of uncertainty

These factors combined mean that you may not be at the exact position on the chart where you have plotted your EP.

You can allow for this by assuming that your position is within a circle of uncertainty which in rough weather and strong tides can be about 10% of the distance travelled.

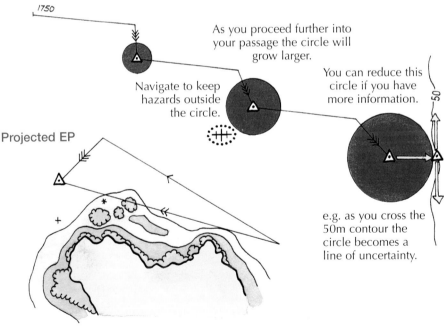

1750

As you proceed further into your passage the circle will grow larger.

You can reduce this circle if you have more information.

Navigate to keep hazards outside the circle.

Projected EP

e.g. as you cross the 50m contour the circle becomes a line of uncertainty.

If you can predict your boatspeed and how the tide will affect you, you can work out a projected in EP (an EP in advance).

This is very useful for calculating your future ground track – "Will I hit the rocks on this heading?" - Yes!

25

Using visual bearings

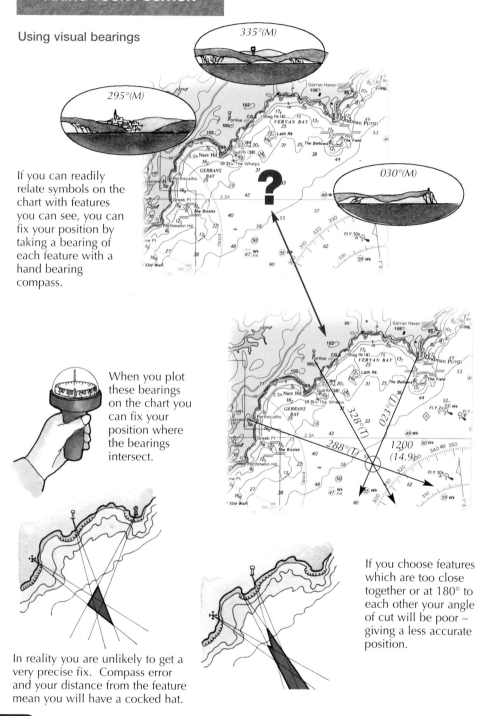

If you can readily relate symbols on the chart with features you can see, you can fix your position by taking a bearing of each feature with a hand bearing compass.

When you plot these bearings on the chart you can fix your position where the bearings intersect.

In reality you are unlikely to get a very precise fix. Compass error and your distance from the feature mean you will have a cocked hat.

If you choose features which are too close together or at 180° to each other your angle of cut will be poor – giving a less accurate position.

When you are moving

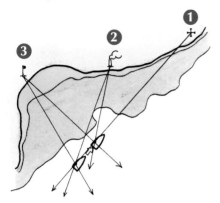

Bearing **1** will change the least – take this first.

Take bearing **2** next.

Bearing **3** will change the most – take this last.

Accuracy

Take care when using buoys for taking a fix - they can move off station in bad weather and their position may change slightly as the tide rises and falls.

When using a hand bearing compass the motion of a boat at sea can make it difficult to obtain a precise fix.

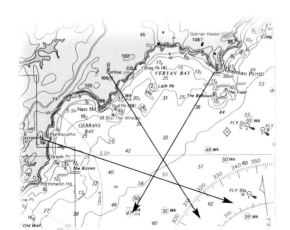

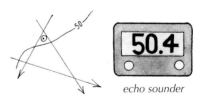

echo sounder

Use other sources of information to help you obtain a more accurate position. Remember with depth information to correct for height of tide.

Simplest fix

This can be taken when passing a charted object.

Transit and Contour

Always allow for the height of tide.

Transit and bearing

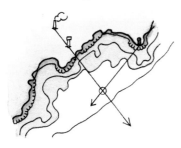

If you use a bearing at about 90° to a transit you will obtain the best angle of cut.

Sector Light

FL(5)WR.20s
17m18/14M

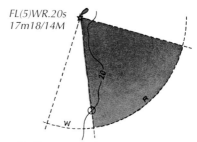

Take a fix if you cross between sectors.

Radar ranges

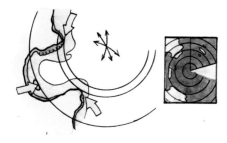

Radar can measure range very accurately. Use 2 or 3 ranges to obtain a fix.

Radar Bearings

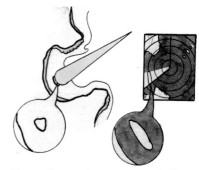

Use with caution as the average radar beam width is 5° or more. The image on the display will seem stretched because of this making the measurement of an exact bearing difficult.

Dipping distance

Use tables from an almanac to give you the range from a lighthouse.

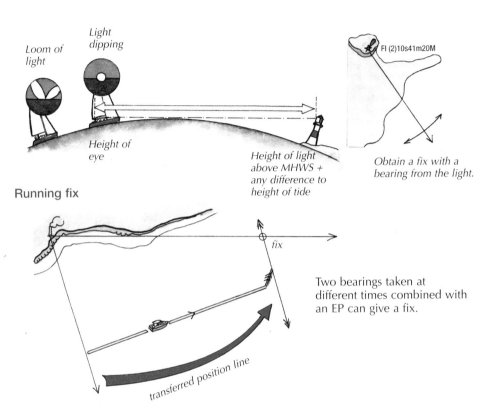

Loom of light

Light dipping

Height of eye

Height of light above MHWS + any difference to height of tide

Fl (2)10s41m20M

Obtain a fix with a bearing from the light.

Running fix

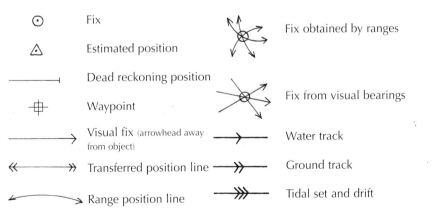

fix

transferred position line

Two bearings taken at different times combined with an EP can give a fix.

PLOTTING SYMBOLS

⊙   Fix

△   Estimated position

———| Dead reckoning position

⊞   Waypoint

————→   Visual fix (arrowhead away from object)

≪————≫   Transferred position line

↙———↗   Range position line

⊗   Fix obtained by ranges

⊗   Fix from visual bearings

——→——   Water track

——≫——   Ground track

——≫≫——   Tidal set and drift

A GPS receiver obtains a fix from signals transmitted by orbiting satellites.

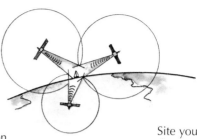

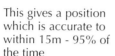

This gives a position which is accurate to within 15m - 95% of the time

Site your aerial low down to avoid signal bounce and thus a less accurate position fix. Ensure it has a clear view of the entire sky and is not shielded in any way.

GPS set-up and display -
some typical features

signal strength

signal status; shows which satellites are in view

make sure the Geodetic datum matches the datum of your current chart.

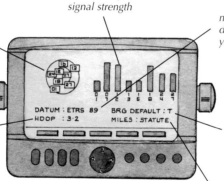

Horizontal Dilution of Precision; when three satellites are too close togeather the fix may be less accurate - as with a visual fix

bearings in °T or °M - you can set as you wish.

ensure that you set this for nautical miles

Low HDoP   *High HDoP*

HDoP
Theoretical best = Value of 1.4
Double figures = poor accuracy.

Waypoints are tools to help you navigate. They are positions stored in the memory of a GPS and used as reference points.

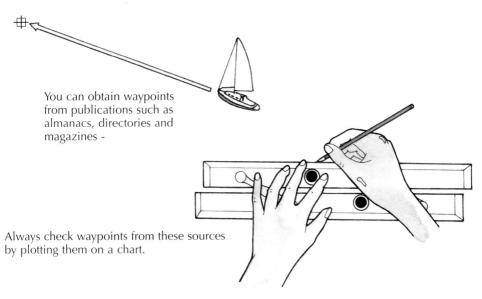

You can obtain waypoints from publications such as almanacs, directories and magazines -

Always check waypoints from these sources by plotting them on a chart.

Be careful when you input a WPT into a GPS. It's as easy to put in the wrong position as it is to dial a wrong phone number.

When you key in a WPT always check that the distance and bearing to WPT given by the GPS matches the distance and bearing that you have measured on the chart.

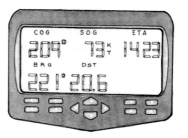

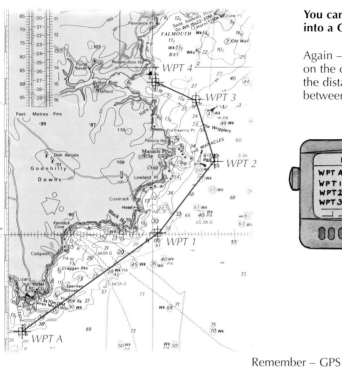

You can enter a series of WPT's into a GPS to make a route.

Again – always plot the WPTS on the chart and double check the distances and bearings between each.

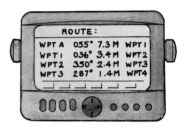

Plot your WPT adjacent to rather than directly on charted objects – you could hit them.

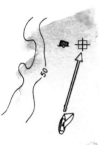

Remember – GPS doesn't allow for tide.

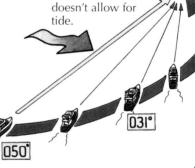

Always pre-plan a course to steer, it's more efficient.

In busy areas, bear in mind that lots of boats could be using the same waypoint.

It seems easy to just steer the bearing that the GPS gives you to a waypoint but if there is much cross tide you:

- sail a longer route
- could put the boat in danger.

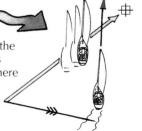

Common terms found on a GPS display

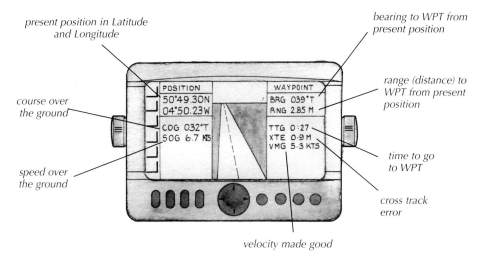

present position in Latitude and Longitude

bearing to WPT from present position

range (distance) to WPT from present position

course over the ground

speed over the ground

time to go to WPT

cross track error

velocity made good

Cross Track Error

This function shows your lateral distance from the Rhumb Line between 2 WPTs

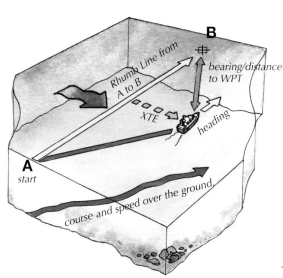

Velocity made good (to WPT)

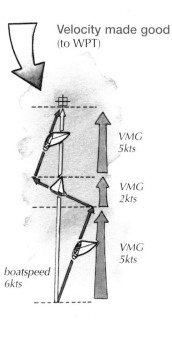

The VMG function shows you your progress towards a waypoint. Here port tack has a higher VMG than starboard.

You can plot your position quickly and simply by entering easily found positions as WPTs. Your GPS will give you a distance and bearing to a WPT and you can plot this to give a fix.

This is easier, quicker and less prone to error than plotting by Latitude and Longitude but double check that you have entered the WPT correctly.

50° 46'.75N
001° 53'.30W

BRG 065
RNG 14.3

Centre of compass rose

Plotter reference on charts.

Intersection of latitude and longitude.

Plotting at speed

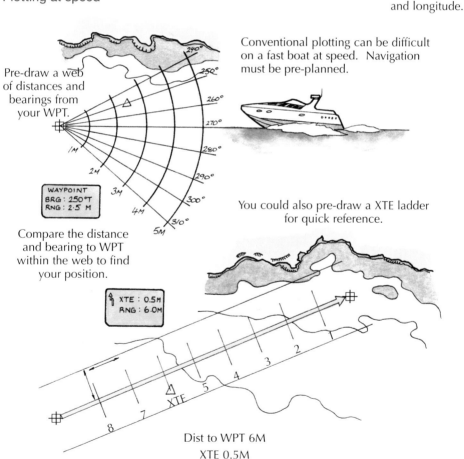

Pre-draw a web of distances and bearings from your WPT.

240°
250°
260°
270°
280°
290°
300°
310°

1M
2M
3M
4M
5M

WAYPOINT
BRG : 250°T
RNG : 2·5 M

Conventional plotting can be difficult on a fast boat at speed. Navigation must be pre-planned.

You could also pre-draw a XTE ladder for quick reference.

Compare the distance and bearing to WPT within the web to find your position.

XTE : 0.5M
RNG : 6.0M

1
2
3
4
5
6
7
8

XTE

Dist to WPT 6M
XTE 0.5M

Plan ahead

Retrospective plotting of your GPS position means you will always be playing catch up.

Pilotage is often a more appropriate method of navigation when you are navigating in close proximity to any hazards.

Reliability

GPS is generally reliable and accurate but as with all electronics it can go wrong, common things to watch out for are:

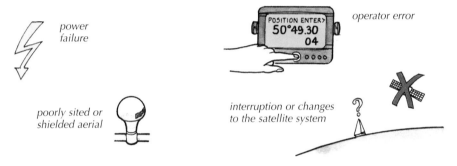

power failure

POSITION ENTER>
50°49.30
04

operator error

poorly sited or shielded aerial

interruption or changes to the satellite system

Back up

Always back up your GPS position with information from another source.

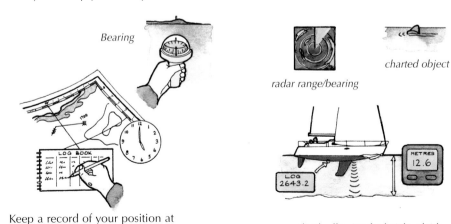

Bearing

radar range/bearing

charted object

LOG BOOK

METRES
12.6

LOG
2643.2

Keep a record of your position at regular intervals on the chart and in the ship's log.

- depth allowing for height of tide
- distance to run

Two main types

Raster charts are the scanned equivalent to a paper chart. They have the same familiar look. Zooming facility is limited compared to vector charts.

Vector charts are produced from layers of information. This means you can select which features you want to show. They are sometimes called 'intelligent charts' as you can set limits and warnings.

PC plotter also used for communications/ tide programs/weather etc.

Electronic chart plotters are interfaced with your GPS to give your position in real time on the screen. WPTs can be managed with the click of a button or mouse.

Dedicated chart plotter using vector charts.

Some plotters combine the use of a paper chart with electronics.

The harsh marine environment and electronics don't always mix well.

- Always carry paper charts with a suitable coverage and an almanac.
- Be aware that your displayed position is from a single source.
- Always back it up with another source of information.
- Keep a separate record of your position.

Depth sounder

Transmits ultrasonic signals which are reflected from the sea bed. Can be less accurate over soft mud and when going astern due to wash from the propeller.

Log

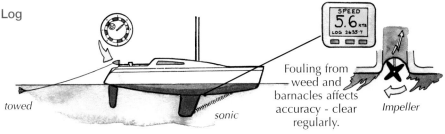

towed

sonic

Fouling from weed and barnacles affects accuracy - clear regularly.

Impeller

Radar

An extremely versatile piece of equipment. Can be used for:

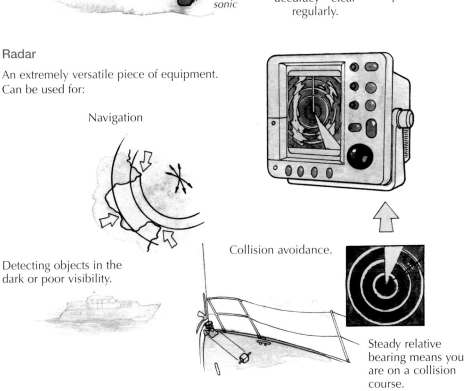

Navigation

Detecting objects in the dark or poor visibility.

Collision avoidance.

Steady relative bearing means you are on a collision course.

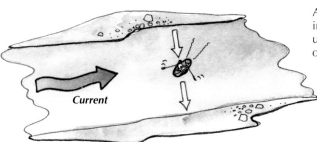

A person rowing across a river instinctively angles the boat upstream to counter the effect of the current.

Current

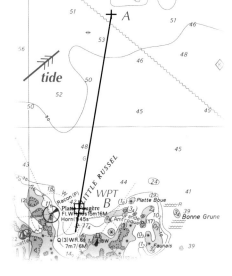

At sea we often can't see our destination so we need to calculate how much to angle into the tidal stream to make the most direct passage.

For example:

If I am at position A at 2100 Wed 17th April, what is the course to steer to waypoint B?

1 How far is it from A to B?

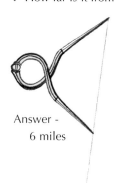

Answer -
6 miles

2 If I think my boat will be capable of 9kn on this passage how long will it take to travel 6 miles?

Answer – roughly an hour because it appears that the tidal stream will push me back.

3 Leaving at 2105 how will the tidal stream affect my passage for the next hour?
Use diamond ⟨K⟩

Wed 17th April HW Plymouth

HW	1835 ⟨
	1905
+1	1935 ⟨
	2005
+2	2035 ⟨
	2105
+3	2135 ⟨
	2205

= 1835 BST
springs

2105 - 2205
= HW +3

Answer 033°(T) 2.3kn

4 Plot the tidal stream at the start of the ground track.

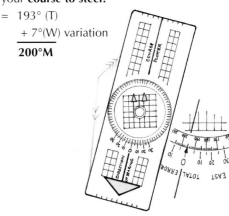

A   033°   2.3kn

5 Measure the expected boat speed for one hour (9kn) and arc dividers from end of tidal stream to cross the ground track, this usually goes beyond or falls short of B, don't worry as long as it's fairly close.

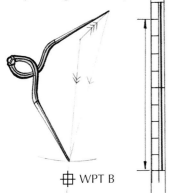

⊞ WPT B

6 Measure bearing of water track - this will be your **course to steer.**

= 193° (T)
+ 7°(W) variation
200°M

Although you are steering 200°(M) your ground track will be the shortest route from A to B

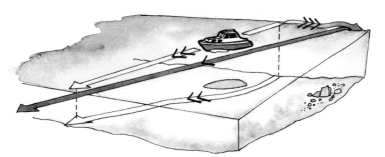

Calculating Estimated Time of Arrival (ETA)

You can work out your ETA to your destination.
How long will it take to get from ⊙ A to ⊞ B?

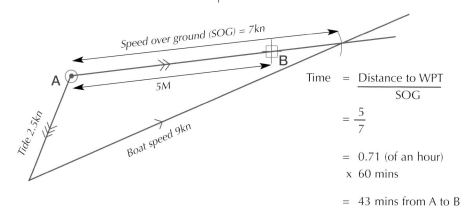

Time = $\dfrac{\text{Distance to WPT}}{\text{SOG}}$

= $\dfrac{5}{7}$

= 0.71 (of an hour)

x 60 mins

= 43 mins from A to B

Vectors

Don't just draw a line from the end of your tidal vector to you destination ('join the dots').

Always arc off the total distance you expect to travel (boatspeed x time) from the end of the tidal vector to a point on your ground track.

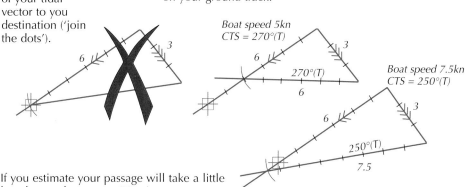

If you estimate your passage will take a little less than an hour – say 50 minutes.

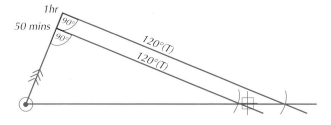

Avoid complicating your calculation by drawing a plot made from say 50 mins of tide and 50 mins of boatspeed.

As long as the predicted tide is constant your answer will be the same as for a 1 hour plot.

When the direction of the tidal streams oppose

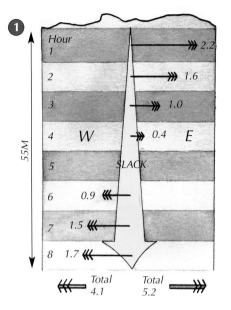

1

Hour	
1	»» 2.2
2	»» 1.6
3	»» 1.0
4	W »» 0.4 E
5	SLACK
6	0.9 ««
7	1.5 ««
8	1.7 ««

55M

«« Total 4.1   Total 5.2 »»

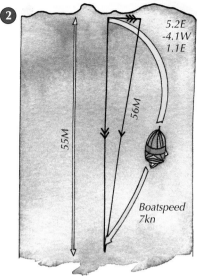

2

5.2E
-4.1W
1.1E

56M

55M

Boatspeed 7kn

Add up all the East and West going tidal streams and plot this as one vector.
Arc off total distance to travel = 7kn x 8 hrs = 56M

When tidal streams change direction every hour

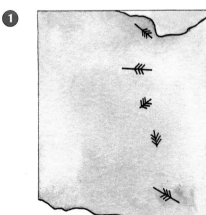

1

You must work out a tidal vector for each hour of passage.

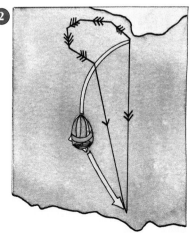

2

Plot chain of vectors at beginning of ground track and then arc off total distance to travel.

A proper look out by sight and sound should be kept at all times.

Beware of blind spots caused by sails/ spray hoods/dodgers etc.

Proceed at a safe speed and beware of faster vessels overtaking.

How can we tell if a risk of collision exists?

1 While on a steady course, take a bearing of the ship or line it up with a part of your boat such as a stanchion or stay.

2 If the bearing of the ship changes or moves in relation to your stanchion there will not be a collision.

If the bearing stays steady a risk of collision exists.

IN ORDER OF PRIORITY

Vessel restricted in ability to manoeuvre (laying marks, dredging etc.)

Vessel constrained by draught

Vessel engaged in fishing

Vessel under sail

Power-driven vessel

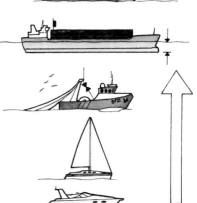

~~ to green should never be green !

IN SIGHT

POWER DRIVEN VESSELS

Head-on

Both vessels turn to
starboard

port to port (red to red)

GIVE WAY

GIVE WAY

A

Crossing

A is on the starboard side of B
B gives way to A

give way to RIGHT STARBOARD

GIVE WAY

B

OVERTAKING

~2 1/2° off bow

Stand-on
vessels must
keep a steady
course and
speed.

Any vessel in
this sector - power or sail -
must give way to the vessel being
overtaken.

GIVE WAY

Give-way vessels must
make their intentions clear,
by making an early, bold
alteration of course.

GIVE WAY

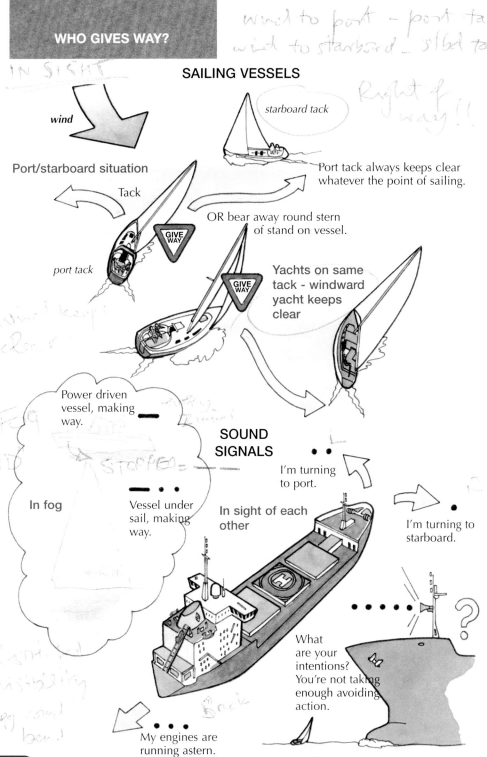

SAILING VESSELS

wind

starboard tack

Port/starboard situation

Tack

Port tack always keeps clear whatever the point of sailing.

OR bear away round stern of stand on vessel.

GIVE WAY

port tack

GIVE WAY

Yachts on same tack - windward yacht keeps clear

Power driven vessel, making way.

SOUND SIGNALS

I'm turning to port.

In fog

Vessel under sail, making way.

In sight of each other

I'm turning to starboard.

What are your intentions? You're not taking enough avoiding action.

My engines are running astern.

TRAFFIC SEPARATION SCHEMES

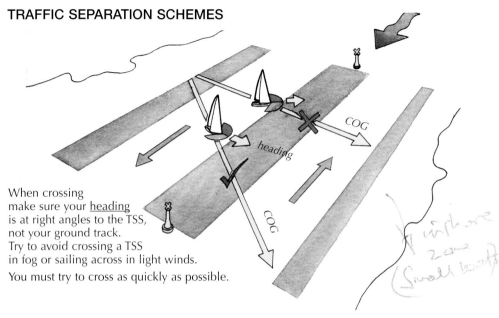

When crossing
make sure your <u>heading</u>
is at right angles to the TSS,
not your ground track.
Try to avoid crossing a TSS
in fog or sailing across in light winds.

You must try to cross as quickly as possible.

NARROW CHANNELS

Power does not necessarily give way to sail when both are navigating in a narrow channel.

Large vessels rely on keeping up their speed to be able to manoeuvre - don't impede them.

If you need to cross a channel your heading should be at 90° to channel.

In most cases small craft can sail outside the main channel – check the chart.

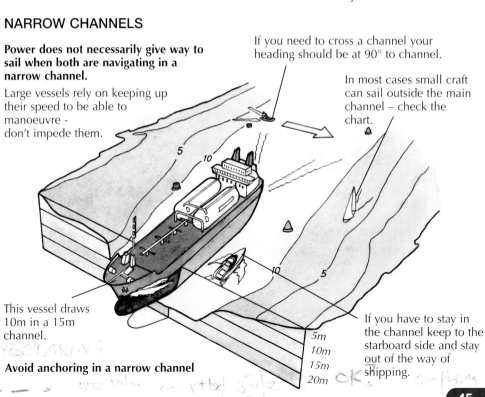

This vessel draws
10m in a 15m
channel.

Avoid anchoring in a narrow channel

5m
10m
15m
20m

If you have to stay in the channel keep to the starboard side and stay out of the way of shipping.

ASPECT LIGHTS

UNDER SAIL

less than 20m

Port

Tricolour light

Stbd

OR

Stern

22.5°

Abaft the beam

Bicolour

Stern light

POWER-DRIVEN VESSELS

Steaming light

Bicolour

Stern light

NEVER switch on steaming light as well as tricolour.

Steaming light

Bicolour

At night

SAILING VESSEL UNDER POWER

By day

motoring cone

Stern light

Stern light

SHIPS

Larger ships (over 50m) must have two steaming lights.

225°

112.5°

135°

112.5°

Starboard view

225°

From astern

From ahead

Port view

For a full explanation of the Collision Regulations see RYA book G2.

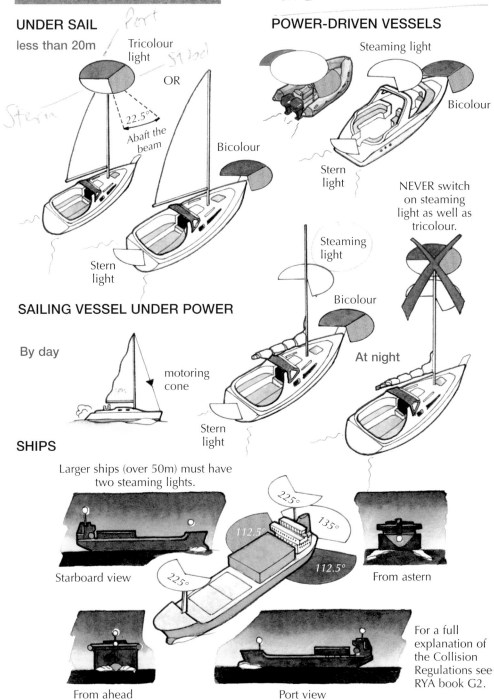

At anchor

Restricted in ability to manoeuvre

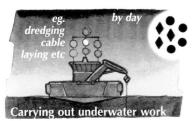

eg. dredging cable laying etc — *by day*

Carrying out underwater work

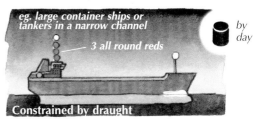

eg. large container ships or tankers in a narrow channel — 3 all round reds — *by day*

Constrained by draught

Fishing trawling

Other types of fishing

by day *by day* white lights have same sector as steaming light

Towing *over 200m* *from astern* *under 200m*

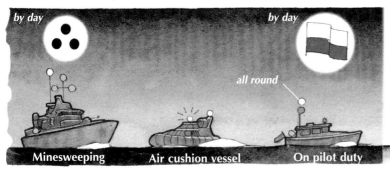

by day *by day* all round

Minesweeping **Air cushion vessel** **On pilot duty**

by day

Diving

For further advice on what safety equipment to carry see RYA book C8 – Cruising Yacht Safety

CG66 form. The coastguard will keep a record of the details of your yacht and a shore contact.

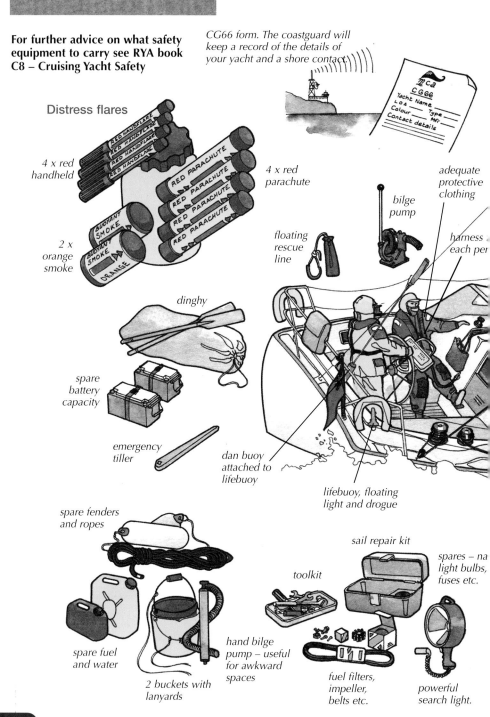

Distress flares

4 x red handheld

4 x red parachute

2 x orange smoke

floating rescue line

bilge pump

adequate protective clothing

harness each per

dinghy

spare battery capacity

emergency tiller

dan buoy attached to lifebuoy

lifebuoy, floating light and drogue

spare fenders and ropes

sail repair kit

toolkit

spares – na light bulbs, fuses etc.

spare fuel and water

hand bilge pump – useful for awkward spaces

2 buckets with lanyards

fuel filters, impeller, belts etc.

powerful search light.

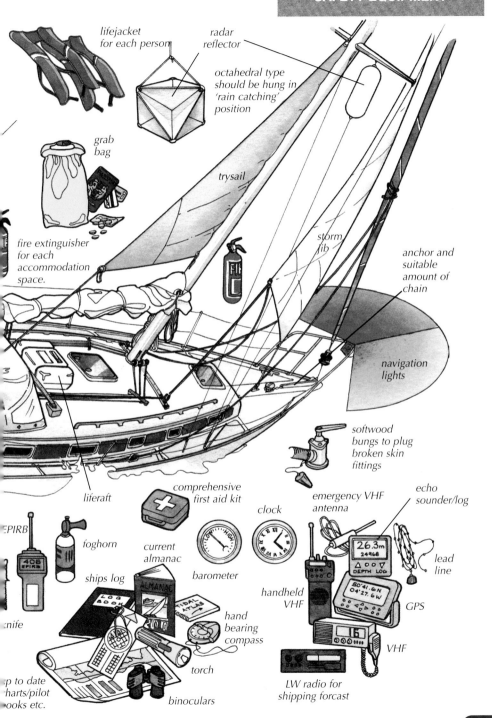

lifejacket for each person

radar reflector

octahedral type should be hung in 'rain catching' position

grab bag

trysail

fire extinguisher for each accommodation space.

storm jib

anchor and suitable amount of chain

navigation lights

softwood bungs to plug broken skin fittings

liferaft

comprehensive first aid kit

clock

emergency VHF antenna

echo sounder/log

EPIRB

foghorn

current almanac

barometer

ships log

handheld VHF

lead line

GPS

:nife

hand bearing compass

VHF

torch

:p to date harts/pilot ooks etc.

binoculars

LW radio for shipping forcast

26.3m
24968
△ O O ▽
DEPTH LOG

50'41.6N
04'27.6W

16

49

Boats return to the upright because of an interaction between their weight and buoyancy.

As a boat heels, B moves away from G creating a righting lever called GZ.

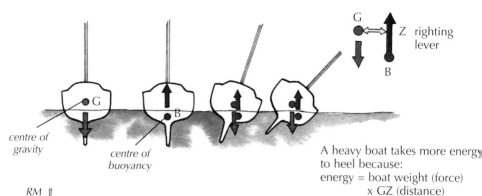

G ⟷ Z righting lever

B

centre of gravity

centre of buoyancy

A heavy boat takes more energy to heel because:

energy = boat weight (force)
         x GZ (distance)
       = RM (righting moment)

RM zero

RM increases to a maximum

30°
60°
90°
120°
150°
180°
0°

as boat heels more - RM decreases

For more information see RYA G23 Yacht Stability.

Angle of Vanishing Stability (AVS) RM is zero. From this point the boat can return to the upright or roll over to be completely inverted.

negative RM makes the boat continue to roll over.

RM zero - stable upside-down

Righting moment curve

Manufacturers produce righting moment curves to show stability characteristics of their boats.

The higher the AVS the more likely a vessel:

- is to resist becoming inverted
- to return to upright after being inverted.

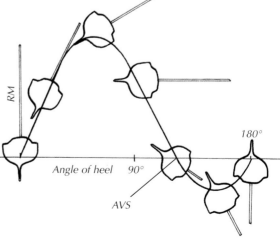

RM

Angle of heel   90°   180°

AVS

Characteristics of different types of yachts

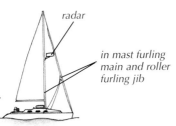

Beamy, light displacement, high volume hull, shallow draft.

Narrow, heavy displacement, low volume hull, deeper draft.

higher AVS

lower AVS

A typical motor cruiser

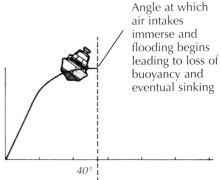

Angle at which air intakes immerse and flooding begins leading to loss of buoyancy and eventual sinking

40°

Raising CoG

Adding weight aloft will raise the centre of gravity and lower your AVS.

radar

in mast furling main and roller furling jib

Breaking waves release large amounts of energy related to their size which in many cases will be sufficient to invert any boat under 24m in length

 AVOID LARGE BREAKING WAVES

Recreational Craft Directive (RCD)

New yachts in Europe are built to the RCD which lays down minimum standards for construction and stability. It gives an indication of the operating limits of a vessel with the category A, B, C, or D displayed on the builders plate.

Category	Wind	Significant Wave height
A Ocean	>F8	>4m
B Offshore	<F8	<4m
C Inshore	<F6	<2m
D Sheltered Waters	<F4	<0.5m

Note - some waves may be twice this height.

A yacht is most likely to be rolled when beam onto a large breaking wave.

When caught beam on, a breaking wave the same height as the beam of your vessel is sufficient to cause it to invert.

Be aware of the limits of your boat when undertaking passages in rough weather and/or where you might encounter breaking waves e.g. tidal overfalls etc.

Common causes of fire

Smoking below decks

Solvents/paints stored below

Gas build-up in the bilges

Faulty wiring

Extinguishers

Dry powder – don't use on flammable liquids.
CO_2 – good for enclosed spaces.
AFFF - foam, good for flammable liquids.

Cooking fats

Petrol vapour

Always vent engine space before starting an inboard petrol engine.

Keep outboards on deck to avoid the build-up of petrol vapour below.

Blanket – good for smothering flames and if clothing is on fire.

Gas safety

Butane and propane can be highly dangerous.

To clear gas - open hatches and turn downwind to vent fresh air through the boat.

Bilge pumps are designed to pump water - many won't clear gas very effectively.

Keep gas bottle in a sealed locker that drains overboard.

Shut-off valve inside near cooker.

Escaping gas is heavier than air and will sink into bilges.

Don't attempt DIY repairs to your system - always call in a qualified fitter.

Location of extinguishers

Automatic for engine space.

Saloon

Forecabin

Extinguishers should be to hand near the exit to each accommodation space.

The engine space should have its own dedicated extinguisher which is automatic or can be activated remotely without having to open the engine compartment and let in oxygen.

Splashing water from a bucket can be more effective than throwing its entire contents at once.

Fighting the fire

Aim the extinguisher at the base of the flames.

Fire blankets can be used to smother a galley fire.

They are also essential for clothing fires.

REMEMBER

The boat will fill up with smoke very quickly.

- Get everyone on deck with a lifejacket.
- You may have to send a Mayday/fire distress flares etc.

If you cannot fight the fire
BE PREPARED TO ABANDON SHIP

Distress flares

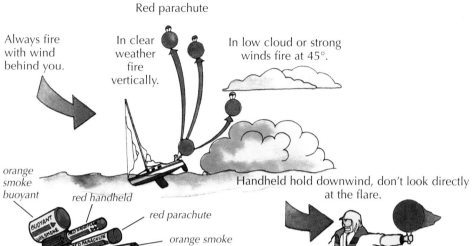

Red parachute

Always fire with wind behind you.

In clear weather fire vertically.

In low cloud or strong winds fire at 45°.

orange smoke buoyant

red handheld

red parachute

orange smoke hand held

Handheld hold downwind, don't look directly at the flare.

Other distress signals

SOS by any means.

Fly a ball under or over a square shape.

Raising and lowering arms.

SART

Search and Rescue Radar Transponder.

Shows your position on another boat's radar.

EPIRB

Emergency Position Indicating Radio Beacon.

When activated it sends a distress message to the rescue services via a satellite system, your position is then pinpointed.

You must register your EPIRB with the coastguard.

VHF VOICE CALL

Use VHF to alert the coastguard and other vessels in your area.

You must tell them:

- your boat's name
- your position
- how many people are on board
- what assistance you require.

VHF is better than a mobile phone for distress calling - other vessels in your area will hear your call and the coastguard can use VHF transmissions to fix your position.

A mobile phone will only tell one person that you are in trouble; the network coverage is patchy away from land and you won't be able to talk direct to a helicopter or lifeboat.

DIGITAL VHF (DSC) CALL

You may not have time to send a voice call but some modern VHF sets can:

- send a distress alert call at the press of a button
- be linked to a GPS to give your position.

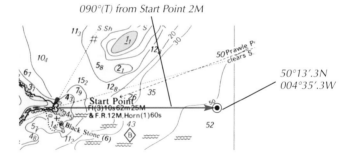

090°(T) from Start Point 2M

50°13'.3N 004°35'.3W

MAYDAY

When life or vessel are in grave and imminent danger

Mayday x 3

This is motor yacht *Puffin* x 3

Mayday yacht *Puffin*

(give MMSI if fitted with DSC)

My position is 50°13'.3N 004°35'.3W

We are holed and sinking and require immediate assistance

Six persons on board

Over

PAN PAN

Urgency message - if crew or vessel need assistance

Pan Pan x 3

All ships x 3

This is yacht *Seaspray* x 3

(give MMSI if fitted with DSC)

My position is 090°(T) from Start Point 4.3 miles

I have a broken rudder and require a tow

Four persons on board

Over

You may use a VHF radio under the supervision of a qualified person or to make a distress call - otherwise you need an operator's certificate. Contact the RYA for details of courses.

Boating is generally a safe pastime but, should the worst happen, make sure you and your crew know what to do.

Use a red parchute or a pinpoint flare (night) or an orange smoke (day).

Put on a lifejacket.

Alert the coast guard.

Activate EPIRB.

ABANDONING TO THE LIFERAFT

Make sure the painter is tied on.

Throw raft to leeward and tug painter to inflate.

Board raft from the yacht. Stay dry.

Put heaviest, strongest crew in first to stabilise the raft and assist others in boarding.

Once aboard:

- cut painter
- paddle away
- stream drogue
- close door
- take seasickness tablets
- keep as warm and dry as possible.

RESCUE BY LIFEBOAT

- The lifeboat coxswain will need to talk to you to assess the situation.
- Make sure there are no lines in the water which could foul the lifeboat's propeller.
  - Any casualties will be taken off.
    - You may be taken in tow but the lifeboat's priority is to save lives not salvage boats.

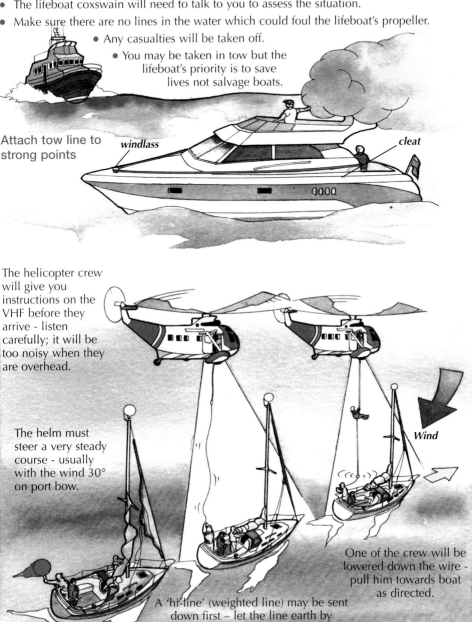

Attach tow line to strong points

windlass

cleat

The helicopter crew will give you instructions on the VHF before they arrive - listen carefully; it will be too noisy when they are overhead.

The helm must steer a very steady course - usually with the wind 30° on port bow.

Wind

One of the crew will be lowered down the wire - pull him towards boat as directed.

A 'hi-line' (weighted line) may be sent down first – let the line earth by touching the water – then gather in slack but don't attach it to the boat.

IALA - A
system

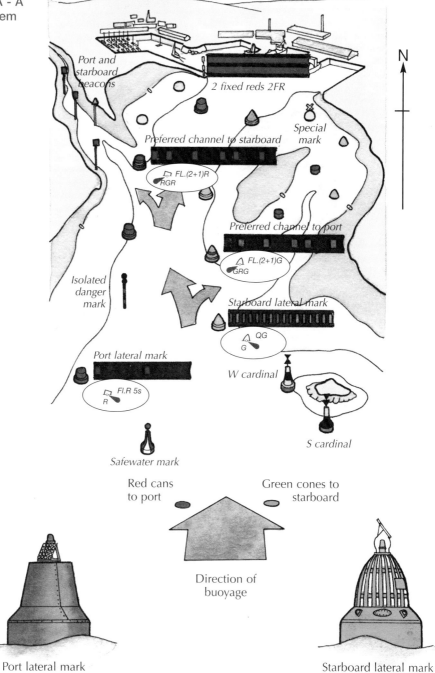

Port and starboard beacons

2 fixed reds 2FR

Preferred channel to starboard

FL.(2+1)R
RGR

Special mark

N

Preferred channel to port

FL.(2+1)G
GRG

Isolated danger mark

Starboard lateral mark

QG
G

Port lateral mark

W cardinal

Fl.R 5s
R

Safewater mark

S cardinal

Red cans
to port

Green cones to
starboard

Direction of
buoyage

Port lateral mark

Starboard lateral mark

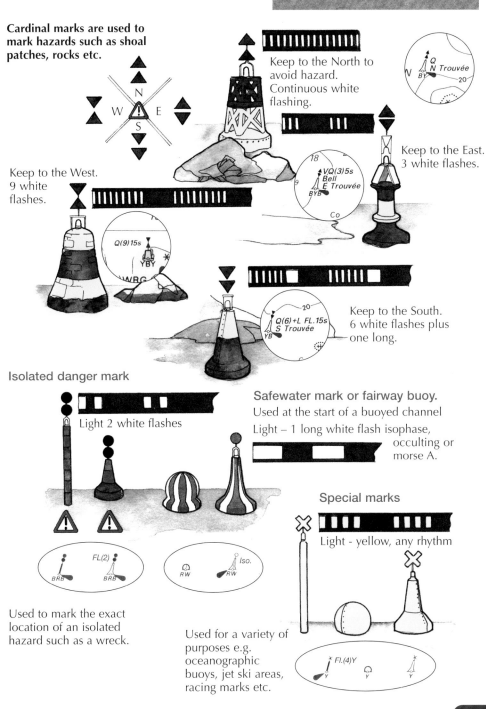

Cardinal marks are used to mark hazards such as shoal patches, rocks etc.

Keep to the North to avoid hazard. Continuous white flashing.

Q N Trouvée
BY 20

Keep to the East. 3 white flashes.

VQ(3)5s Bell E Trouvée BYB

Keep to the West. 9 white flashes.

Q(9)15s YBY

Keep to the South. 6 white flashes plus one long.

Q(6)+L FL.15s S Trouvée YB

Isolated danger mark

Light 2 white flashes

Used to mark the exact location of an isolated hazard such as a wreck.

FL(2)
BRB   *BRB*

Safewater mark or fairway buoy.
Used at the start of a buoyed channel
Light – 1 long white flash isophase, occulting or morse A.

Iso.
RW   *RW*

Special marks

Light - yellow, any rhythm

Used for a variety of purposes e.g. oceanographic buoys, jet ski areas, racing marks etc.

FL.(4)Y
Y   *Y*   *Y*

Light characteristics

Oc		Occulting (more light than dark)
Fl		Single flashing
Fl.(3)		Group flashing
F		Fixed
Iso		Isophase (equal light and dark)

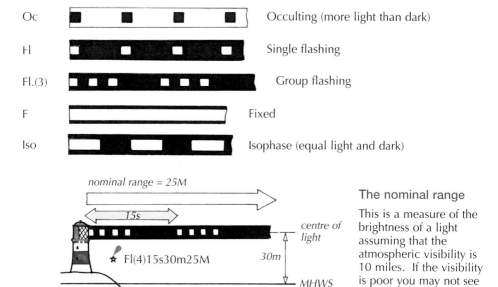

The nominal range

This is a measure of the brightness of a light assuming that the atmospheric visibility is 10 miles. If the visibility is poor you may not see the light until you are much closer.

nominal range = 25M

15s

centre of light

30m

MHWS

★ Fl(4)15s30m25M

Nominal range does not account for the curvature of the earth; you won't be able to see a light unless you have a direct line of sight to it above the horizon.

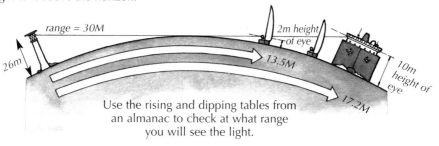

range = 30M

2m height of eye

26m

13.5M

10m height of eye

17.2M

Use the rising and dipping tables from an almanac to check at what range you will see the light.

Table 2 (2) Lights - distance off when rising or dipping (M)											
Height of light		*yacht*				**Height of eye**					*ship*
		metres	1	2	3	4	5	6	7	8	9	10
metres	feet	feet	3	7	10	13	16	20	23	26	30	33
24	79		12.3	13.1	13.8	14.4	14.9	15.3	15.7	16.1	16.4	17.0
26	85		12.7	13.5	14.2	14.8	15.3	15.7	16.1	16.5	16.8	17.2
28	92		13.1	13.9	14.6	15.2	15.7	16.1	16.5	16.9	17.2	17.6

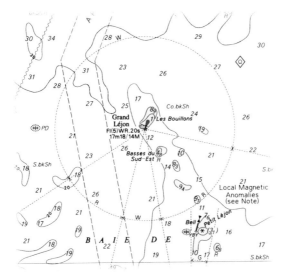

Sector lights are designed to help you avoid danger by casting a sector of coloured light over a hazard or dangerous approach.

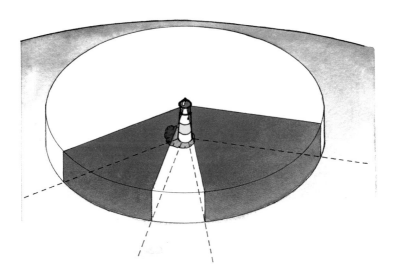

A single structure may show several lights with different nominal ranges.

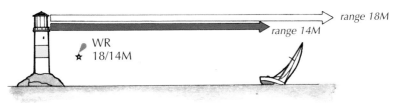

range 18M

range 14M

WR
18/14M

LEADING LIGHTS

The orientation of leading lights usually suggests which way you should turn to enter or leave harbour on the recommended ground track.

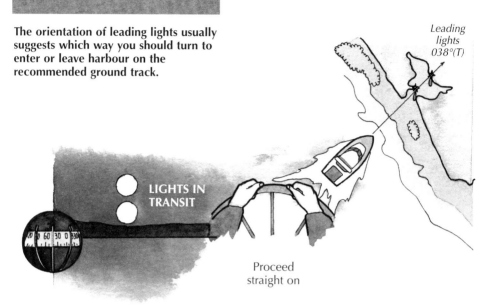

Leading lights 038°(T)

LIGHTS IN TRANSIT

Proceed straight on

TOO FAR TO PORT

Turn to starboard

Turn to port

TOO FAR TO STARBOARD

Directional lights help guide you in and out of harbour by using narrow sectors of colour.

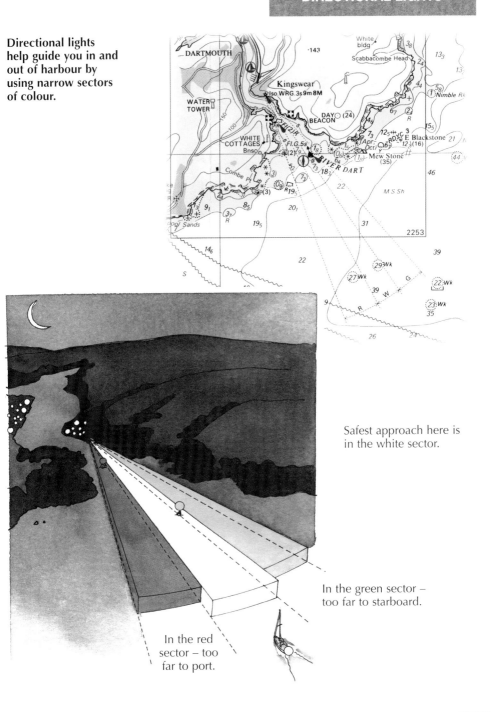

Safest approach here is in the white sector.

In the green sector – too far to starboard.

In the red sector – too far to port.

Pilotage is the art of inshore navigation when you have visual references to help you find your way along the coast and in and out of harbour.

There may be lots of different hazards so good planning is essential.

THINGS YOU MIGHT NEED TO PLAN FOR

Rocks

Shoals & shallows

Shipping channels

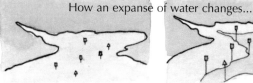
How an expanse of water changes...

at high water   and low water

Chain ferries

Harbour byelaws

e.g. Small craft channels

SPEED LIMIT (5) IN HARBOUR

Speed restriction in channel

Effect of tide

INTERNATIONAL PORT TRAFFIC SIGNALS

Serious emergency do not proceed

Do not proceed (waiting for lock)

Proceed one way traffic (e.g. entering a lock)

Proceed two way traffic (e.g. lock freeflow)

Await orders to proceed

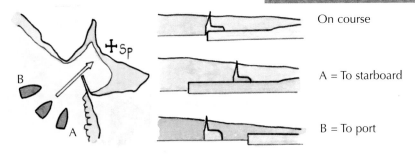

On course

A = To starboard

B = To port

Contours

You can work out where you are when you cross a contour and they can be followed in poor visibility.

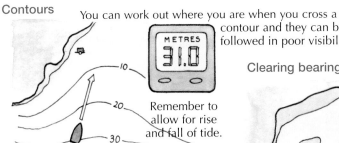

Remember to allow for rise and fall of tide.

Clearing bearing

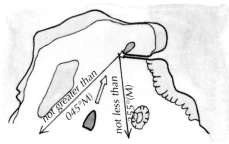

You can go anywhere between the two bearings.

Back bearings

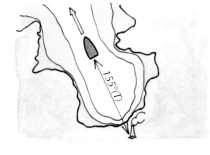

Bearing + distance

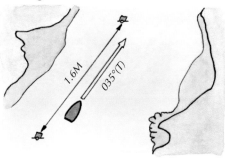

Work this out in advance so you know when and where to expect the next buoy

Turning points

Turn when chimney bears 320°(T)

To navigate safely in congested inshore waters it is best to spend as much time as possible on deck. This means you are able to:

- keep an eye out for other vessels
- make sure that the yacht stays on the required ground track, using visual references.

The best way to achieve this is to make a plan in advance for example:

Passage Sark to Beaucette (Guernsey) 8th July.

- Look up the tide times and calculate at what time you can clear the sill at Beaucette.

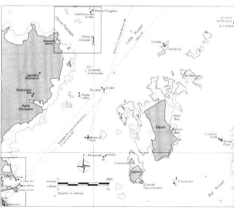

- Use chart and information from an almanac/pilot book to produce a pilotage plan.

By making a sketch you can extract the essential details of
your plan to keep handy when on deck.

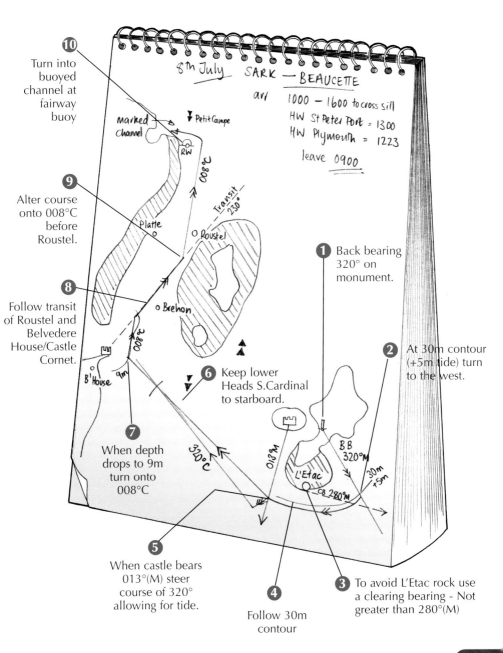

10 Turn into buoyed channel at fairway buoy

9 Alter course onto 008°C before Roustel.

8 Follow transit of Roustel and Belvedere House/Castle Cornet.

7 When depth drops to 9m turn onto 008°C

6 Keep lower Heads S.Cardinal to starboard.

5 When castle bears 013°(M) steer course of 320° allowing for tide.

4 Follow 30m contour

3 To avoid L'Etac rock use a clearing bearing - Not greater than 280°(M)

2 At 30m contour (+5m tide) turn to the west.

1 Back bearing 320° on monument.

Within the sketch (handwritten):

8th July   SARK — BEAUCETTE

avl   1000 — 1600 to cross sill
HW St Peter Port = 1300
HW Plymouth = 1223

leave 0900

Petit Caunpe
Marked Channel
RW
008°C
Transit 230°
Platte
o Roustel
o Brehon
B'House
9m
008°C
320°C
013°M
L'Etac
CB 280°M
BB 320°M
30m +5m

TYPES OF ANCHOR

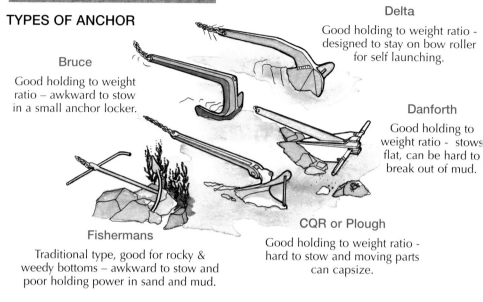

Delta
Good holding to weight ratio - designed to stay on bow roller for self launching.

Bruce
Good holding to weight ratio – awkward to stow in a small anchor locker.

Danforth
Good holding to weight ratio - stows flat, can be hard to break out of mud.

Fishermans
Traditional type, good for rocky & weedy bottoms – awkward to stow and poor holding power in sand and mud.

CQR or Plough
Good holding to weight ratio - hard to stow and moving parts can capsize.

SCOPE

The scope of chain or warp you need depends on the maximum depth of water you expect during your stay.

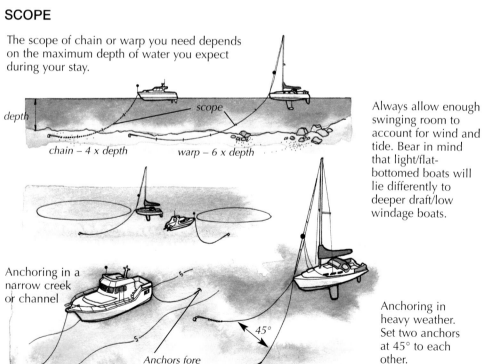

depth

scope

chain – 4 x depth *warp – 6 x depth*

Always allow enough swinging room to account for wind and tide. Bear in mind that light/flat-bottomed boats will lie differently to deeper draft/low windage boats.

Anchoring in a narrow creek or channel

Anchors fore and aft

45°

Anchoring in heavy weather. Set two anchors at 45° to each other.

Selecting an anchor berth

Some points to consider:

- Shelter from wind/swell/tidal stream
- Tidal rise and fall
- Nature of the seabed
- Swinging room-other boats/hazards etc.

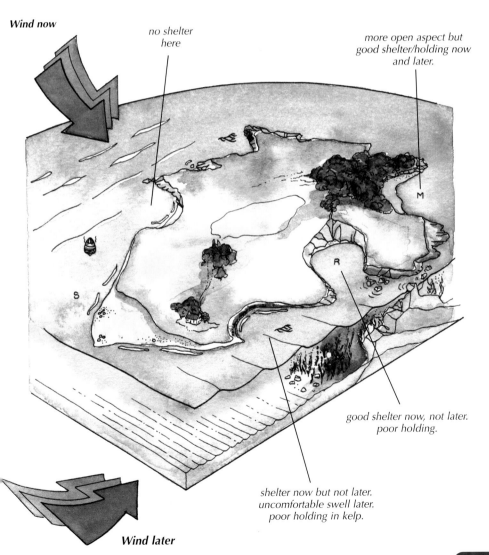

Wind now

no shelter
here

more open aspect but
good shelter/holding now
and later.

good shelter now, not later.
poor holding.

shelter now but not later.
uncomfortable swell later.
poor holding in kelp.

Wind later

Basic principles

The driving force behind our weather is the distribution and movement of energy from the sun around the earth.

As the sun heats the earth – hot air rises and is replaced by cold air, rather like a bonfire.

Warmer air:

- is lighter and less dense than cold air.
- can hold more moisture than cold air.

Colder air:

- is heavier and denser than warm air.
- can hold less moisture than warm air.

Air will always try to move from an area of higher pressure to an area of lower pressure.

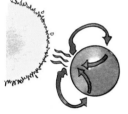

In very simple terms – hot air at the equator rises and is replaced by cooler air moving in from elsewhere.

In reality the situation is more complex because of the unequal distribution of land and water.

The oceans act like giant storage heaters.

Ocean Currents move warm and cold water to different parts of the globe.

Winter   Summer

Heat distribution round the world changes with the seasons.

Coriolis effect

The spin of the earth causes air to be deflected as it moves around the earth.

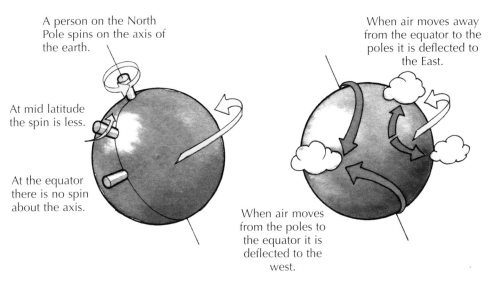

A person on the North Pole spins on the axis of the earth.

At mid latitude the spin is less.

At the equator there is no spin about the axis.

When air moves away from the equator to the poles it is deflected to the East.

When air moves from the poles to the equator it is deflected to the west.

A combination of all these effects leads to complex weather patterns.

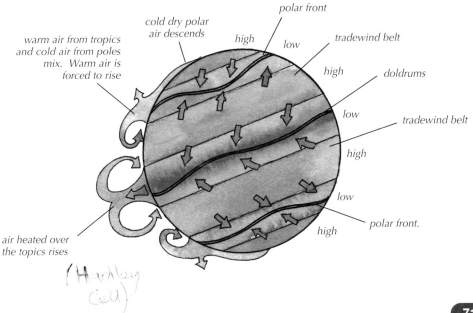

warm air from tropics and cold air from poles mix. Warm air is forced to rise

cold dry polar air descends

polar front

high

low

tradewind belt

high

doldrums

low

tradewind belt

high

low

air heated over the topics rises

polar front.

high

(Hadley Cell)

Unstable = hot air rising
Stable = cold air sinking

Formation of a depression

In the UK much of our weather is determined by Atlantic depressions - areas of low pressure which typically give strong or gale force winds and rain. They are formed at the Polar Front – the junction between cold air moving away from the poles and warm air moving away from the tropics.

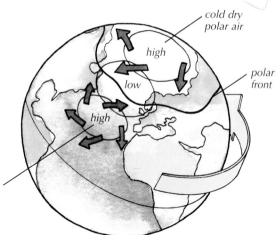

cold dry polar air

high

polar front

low

high

warm moist tropical air

Early stages

Imagine the polar high and the tropical high as two clockwise turning cogs.

Clockwise turning cogs can't mesh causing friction.

You could think of a depression as the anticlockwise cog that fits between the two.

Progression

The depression is made up from rising warm air and descending cold air. It starts to spin.

The warm air rises over the cold air.

The cold air forces its way beneath the warm air.

The cold dry air meets the warm moist air at fronts – these are like battle zones between the two different types of air.

Warm air rises.
Depression deepens.

warm front

cold front

How a depression matures

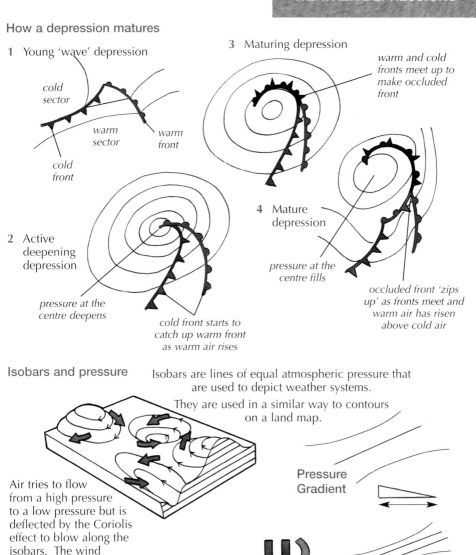

1 Young 'wave' depression

cold sector

warm sector

warm front

cold front

3 Maturing depression

warm and cold fronts meet up to make occluded front

4 Mature depression

2 Active deepening depression

pressure at the centre deepens

pressure at the centre fills

cold front starts to catch up warm front as warm air rises

occluded front 'zips up' as fronts meet and warm air has risen above cold air

Isobars and pressure

Isobars are lines of equal atmospheric pressure that are used to depict weather systems.

They are used in a similar way to contours on a land map.

Air tries to flow from a high pressure to a low pressure but is deflected by the Coriolis effect to blow along the isobars. The wind measured from the alignment and distance apart of the isobars is known as the pressure gradient wind.

Pressure Gradient

Buys Ballot's Law

In the Northern Hemisphere if you stand with your back to the wind, the low pressure system will be on your left hand side and the high pressure on your right.

The closer together the isobars – the stronger the wind

FEATURES OF A TYPICAL DEPRESSION, IN THE NORTHERN HEMISPHERE.

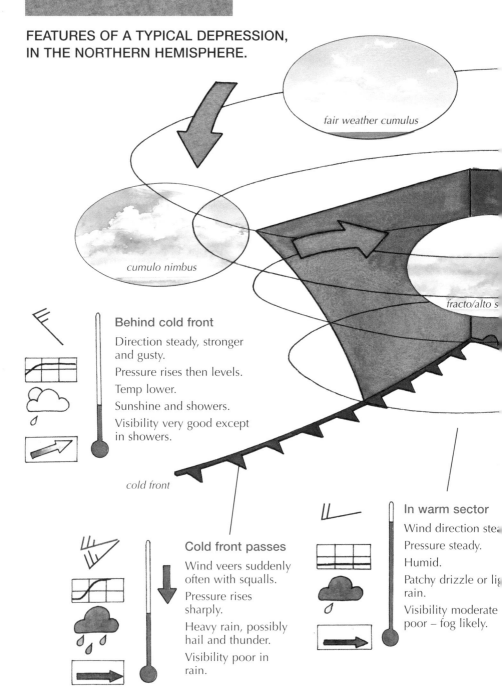

fair weather cumulus

cumulo nimbus

fracto/alto s

Behind cold front

Direction steady, stronger and gusty.

Pressure rises then levels.

Temp lower.

Sunshine and showers.

Visibility very good except in showers.

cold front

Cold front passes

Wind veers suddenly often with squalls.

Pressure rises sharply.

Heavy rain, possibly hail and thunder.

Visibility poor in rain.

In warm sector

Wind direction ste

Pressure steady.

Humid.

Patchy drizzle or li rain.

Visibility moderate poor – fog likely.

veer = clockwise
back - anti clockwise

Cirro
Alto
Cumulus
Stratus - layer

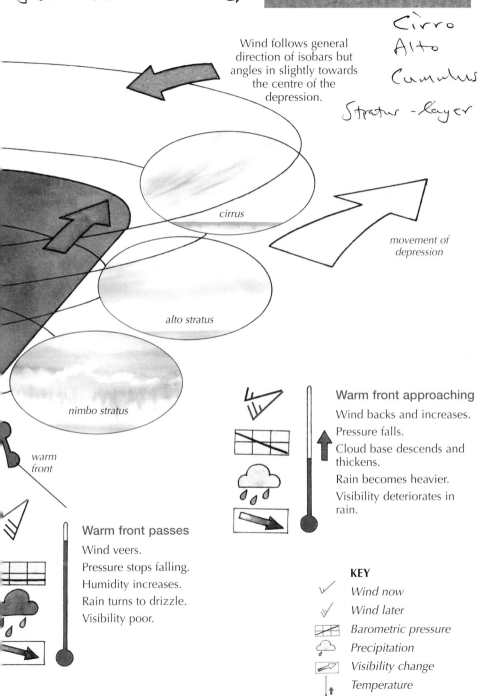

Wind follows general direction of isobars but angles in slightly towards the centre of the depression.

cirrus

movement of depression

alto stratus

nimbo stratus

warm front

Warm front approaching

Wind backs and increases.
Pressure falls.
Cloud base descends and thickens.
Rain becomes heavier.
Visibility deteriorates in rain.

Warm front passes

Wind veers.
Pressure stops falling.
Humidity increases.
Rain turns to drizzle.
Visibility poor.

KEY

✓	*Wind now*
✓	*Wind later*
⊞	*Barometric pressure*
☁	*Precipitation*
◨	*Visibility change*
┃	*Temperature*

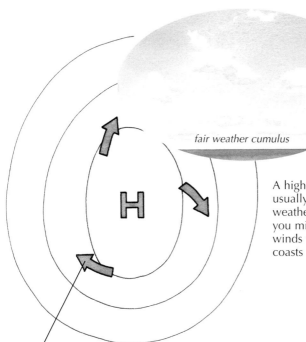

fair weather cumulus

A high pressure or anticyclone is usually associated with fine settled weather and light winds. However, you might experience locally strong winds which have been funnelled by coasts and mountains.

wind flows clockwise around a high pressure in the northern hemisphere and away from its centre

Land breeze

Sea breeze

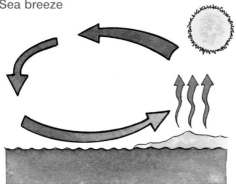

In fair weather and light to moderate offshore wind, a sea breeze is likely to develop. Warm air rises over land, it then cools, descends and blows onshore. Wind up to force 4 in strength.

This occurs on a clear night when the air cools over land and flows downhill and out to sea, particularly from river estuaries.
Wind usually no more than force 2- 3 except near mountains.

T ort tack coming to [?]

Local winds

Wind often varies significantly from the forecast or gradient wind.

Wind is slowed down by friction which is greater over land than sea.

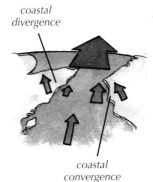

coastal divergence

+

when wind slows – Coriolis force causes it to back

coastal convergence

When near the coast:

- wind on your back, land on your right - expect stronger wind
- wind on your back, land on your left - expect lighter wind.

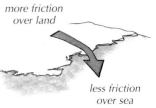

more friction over land

less friction over sea

Wind blowing offshore can be fluky in direction and strength – especially when blowing off trees, buildings, cliffs etc.

Wind is more backed over land than sea

If the wind is blowing off the land expect it to back as you approach the coast.

FOG

Advection or sea fog

This occurs when warm moist air blows over a colder sea. It is usually associated

with the warm S or SW winds of a depression. It is most common in spring when sea temperature is at its lowest.

Radiation or land fog

Usually occurs in settled weather in autumn/winter. Land cools down quickly at night. Moisture condenses and forms fog over land which will drift out to sea on the land breeze.

Shipping Forecast Areas

There are many different ways to obtain a forecast:

- Marine safety information broadcasts on VHF by Coastguard.
- Metfax
- Short message service (SMS)
- Recorded forecasts by phone
- Internet
- Teletext
- Many harbour and marina offices post a forecast.
- Local radio stations.
- Navtex

For details of forecast times etc. look in an almanac or RYA book of Weather Forecasts (G5)

TERMS USED IN FORECASTS

Gale	If average wind is expected to be F8 or more or gusts 43-51kn.
Strong wind warnings	If average wind is expected to be F6 or F7. F6 is often called a yachtsman's gale.
Timing	*Imminent* - Within 6 hours from time of issue of warning or forecast.
	Soon - Within 6-12 hours of time of issue of warning or forecast.
	Later - More than 12 hours from time of issue of warning or forecast.
Visibility	*Good* - greater than 5 miles *Moderate* - between 2 - 5 miles. *Poor* - 1,000m to 2 miles. Fog less than 1,000m.
Fair	No significant precipitation.
Backing	Wind changing in an anticlockwise direction eg NW to SW.
Veering	Wind changing in a clockwise direction eg NE to SE.
General synopsis	How, when and where the weather systems are moving.
Sea states	*Smooth* - wave height 0.2 - 0.5m *Slight* - wave height 0.5 - 1.25m *Moderate* - wave height 1.25 - 2.5m *Rough* - wave height 2.5 - 4m *Very rough* - wave height 4 - 6m.
Pressure and Tendency	*Steady* - Change less than 0.1mb in 3 hours *Rising or falling slowly* - change 0.1 - 1.5mb in last 3 hours *Rising or falling* - change 1.6 - 3.5mb in last 3 hours *Rising or falling quickly* - change 3.6 - 6.0mb in last 3 hours *Rising or falling very rapidly* - change of more than 6.0mb in last 3 hours *Now falling, now rising* - change from rising to falling or vice versa within the last 3 hours

1 **Light airs** 1 - 3 knots
Ripples.
Sail - drifting conditions
Power - fast planing conditions

2 **Light breeze** 4 - 6 knots
Small wavelets.
Sail - full mainsail and large genoa
Power - fast planing conditions

3 **Gentle breeze** 7 - 10 knots
Occasional crests.
Sail - full sail
Power - fast planing conditions

4 **Moderate** 11 - 16 knots
Frequent white horses.
Sail - reduce headsail size
Power - may have to slow down if wind
against tide

5 **Fresh breeze** 17 - 21 knots
Moderate waves, many white crests.
Sail - reef mainsail
Power - reduce speed to prevent slamming
when going upwind

6 **Strong breeze** 22 - 27 knots
Large waves, white foam crests.
Sail - reef main and reduce headsail
Power - displacement speed

7 **Near gale** 28 - 33 knots
Sea heaps up, spray, breaking waves, foam
blows in streaks.
Sail - deep reefed main, small jib
Power - displacement speed

8 **Gale** 34 - 40 knots
Moderately high waves, breaking crests.
Sail - deep reefed main, storm jib
Power - displacement speed, stem waves

9 **Severe gale** 41 - 47 knots
High waves, spray affects visibility.
Sail - trysail and storm jib
Power - displacement speed, stem waves

10 **Storm** 48 - 55 knots
Very high waves, long breaking crests.
Survival conditions

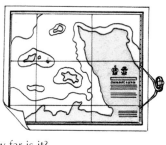

2 What time do we need to arrive?

1 How far is it?

3 What is the weather forecast?

4 How long will the passage take?

Progress upwind can be slow and uncomfortable

Down wind - you can steer a more direct course and make good progress.

Boat speed 18 knots - Distance 60 miles = $3\frac{1}{2}$ hours
Boat speed 6 knots - Distance 60 miles = 10 hours
will any of these hours be in darkness?

5 Tidal gates

The fastest passage in a sailing boat is in a favourable tide - this could mean rougher water

Motor yachts are faster in a flat sea, even if this means a passage against the tide.

6 Course to steer

What allowances must be made for tide?

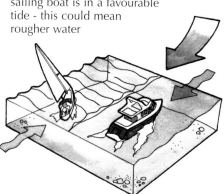

7 What hazards will be encountered en route?

8 Prepare pilotage plan for departure and entry, preparing for arrival in darkness.

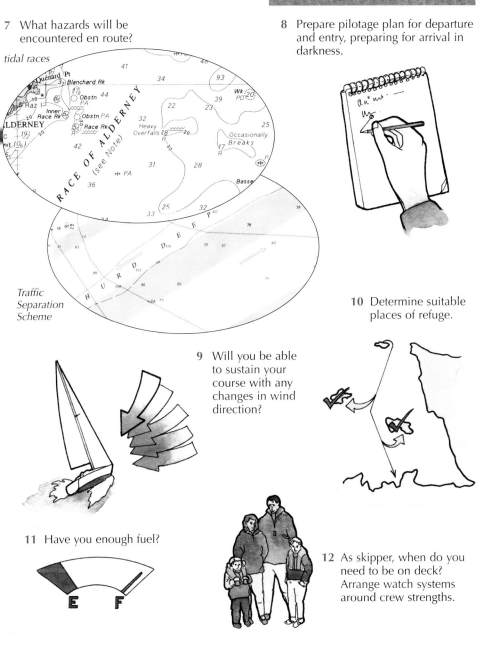

tidal races

Traffic Separation Scheme

10 Determine suitable places of refuge.

9 Will you be able to sustain your course with any changes in wind direction?

11 Have you enough fuel?

12 As skipper, when do you need to be on deck? Arrange watch systems around crew strengths.

13 Is the passage within the limits of you, your crew and your boat?

It is not advisable to set out in fog, especially if you don't have a radar set.
However if you are caught out:

- Fix your position

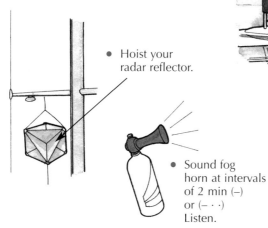

- Hoist your radar reflector.

- Sound fog horn at intervals of 2 min (–) or (– · ·) Listen.

- Muster crew on deck in life jackets.

- Listen on Port frequency to check for commercial traffic.

- If you have radar keep a constant experienced radar watch.

Navigation strategy

1 Get out of shipping lanes

2 Find and follow contour in.

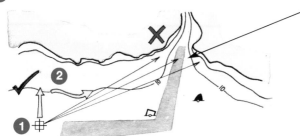

Where possible, don't set a course directly for the entrance to a port.

Error might take you to the wrong side and you might put yourself directly in the path of commercial vessels.

Rules of the road "Highway Code"   (CEVNi test for Europe)

anywhere anchored or connected to sea by cannal.

good responsibility to avoid collision.

idling but running under engine => motor vessel

"not under command" = broken down.

"restricted ability to manoeuvre" = eg fishing boat, laying pipes or underwater ops

"constrained by draft" ie big ships.

"underway" - state of being not tied up @ anchor, aground

"making way" - underway under power/steering   steering

"in sight" - if can be visually observed (not radar)

"proper look out" - looking, hearing, all round.

— look behind sails - radar on + use it.

"safe speed" - visibility, traffic density, manoeuvrability, weather, noting tide beyond draft available beyond light @ night

"constant bearing" leads to collision.

"risk of collision" - avoid - pointing in good time, with good seamanship → make it obvious

@ night - alter course to show different light.

"narrow channel" keep to RIGHT (port to port)

Tug = — • • TENDER/   — • • •
             BARGE/

sailing vessel @ anchor — make a noise
motor boat < 100m — bell / every (2 mins)
            > 100m bell @ front, gong @ stern.

+ • — • 3 short bell,
aground — bell, gong, whistle

pilot boat • • • •

Restricted visibility - safe speed, engines ready to move
fog-detect by radar - risk of collision exists (ARPA-AutoRadar Plotting
⟹ don't turn to port, towards vessel

RYA Membership

Promoting and Protecting Boating
www.rya.org.uk

RYA

The RYA is the national
organisation which
represents the interests
of everyone who goes
boating for pleasure.

The greater the membership, the
louder our voice when it comes to
protecting members' interests.

Apply for membership today,
and support the RYA, to help
the RYA support you.

nd Protecting Boating

Benefits of Membership

- Access to expert advice on all aspects of boating from legal wrangles to training matters

- Special members' discounts on a range of products and services including boat insurance, books, videos and class certificates

- Free issue of certificates of competence, increasingly asked for by everyone from overseas governments to holiday companies, insurance underwriters to boat hirers

- Access to the wide range of RYA publications, including the quarterly magazine

- Third Party insurance for windsurfing members

- Free Internet access with RYA-Online

- Special discounts on AA membership

- Regular offers in RYA Magazine

- ...and much more

Join online at *www.rya.org.uk* or use the form overleaf.

Visit the website for information, advice, member services and web shop.

If you have previously been a member and know your membership number please enter here

When completed, please send this form to: RYA RYA House Ensign Way Hamble Southampton SO31 4YA

	Tick box	Cash/Chq.	DD
Family†		£44	£41
Personal		£28	£25
Under 21		£11	£11

Please indicate your main area of interest

❏ Yacht Racing   ❏ Dinghy Cruising
❏ Yacht Cruising   ❏ Personal Watercraft
❏ Dinghy Racing   ❏ Inland Waterways

❏ Powerboat Racing
❏ Windsurfing
❏ Motor Boating
❏ Sportsboats and RIBs

These prices are valid until 30.10.03   † Family Membership = 2 adults plus any U21s all living at the same address.

For details of Life Membership and paying over the phone by Credit/Debit card, please call 0845 345 0374/5 or join online at www.rya.org.uk

PLEASE USE BLOCK CAPITALS

	Title	Forename	Surname	Date of Birth	Male	Female
1.						
2.						
3.						
4.						

Address

Town ___   County ___   Postcode ___

Home Phone No. ___   Day Phone No. ___

Facsimile No. ___   Mobile No. ___

Email Address ___

Signature ___   Date ___

RYA

Instructions to your Bank or Building Society to pay by Direct Debit

DIRECT Debit

Please fill in the form and send to:
RYA RYA House Ensign Way Hamble Southampton SO31 4YA Tel: 0845 345 0400

Name and full postal address of your Bank/Building Society

To The Manager	Bank/Building Society
Address	
	Postcode

Name(s) of Account Holder(s)

Bank/Building Society account number

Branch Sort Code

Originator's Identification Number

9	5	5	2	1	3

Reference Number

Instruction to your Bank or Building Society
Please pay Royal Yachting Association Direct Debits from the account detailed in this instruction subject to the safeguards assured by The Direct Debit Guarantee. I understand that this instruction may remain with the Royal Yachting Association and, if so, details will be passed electronically to my Bank/Building Society.

Signature(s)

Date

Banks and Building Societies may not accept Direct Debit Instructions for some types of account

---

OR YOU CAN PAY BY CHEQUE

Source Code		
077		

Cheque enclosed   £   Made payable to the Royal Yachting Association

Office use only: Membership number allocated